Laura Waters is a freelance travel writer and speaker with a passion for inspiring people to connect with nature. Committed to leading a life less ordinary, she has lived in various places around the globe while squeezing in random adventures such as mountain biking coast to coast across England or sailing 700 kilometres up the Queensland coast.

In 2009 Laura trained with Al Gore to be a climate presenter, educating people about the challenges of and solutions to climate change.

She is loosely based in Melbourne but is usually found roaming with a backpack and laptop in search of adventures. Visit her at www.soultrekkers.com.au

BEWILDERED

Affirmpress
books that leave an impression

Published by Affirm Press in 2019
28 Thistlethwaite Street, South Melbourne, VIC 3205
www.affirmpress.com.au
10 9 8 7 6 5 4 3 2 1

Title: Bewildered / Laura Waters, author
ISBN: 9781925870541 (paperback)

 A catalogue record for this
book is available from the
National Library of Australia

Cover design by Affirm Press
Photographs © Laura Waters
Typeset by J&M Typesetting Baskerville 12.5 / 18.75
Proudly printed in Australia by Griffin Press

MIX
Paper from
responsible sources
FSC® C009448

The paper this book is printed on is certified against the Forest Stewardship
Council® Standards. Griffin Press holds FSC chain of custody certification
SGS-COC-005088. FSC promotes environmentally responsible, socially
beneficial and economically viable management of the world's forests.

This book is mostly about hiking the Te Araroa Trail, however the cover
image was taken on another trail 40km west of Te Araroa, near Wanaka in the
South Island. This route features in the epilogue.

Laura Waters

BE**WILD**ERED

Leaving everything behind for
3000km in the wilds of New Zealand

Contents

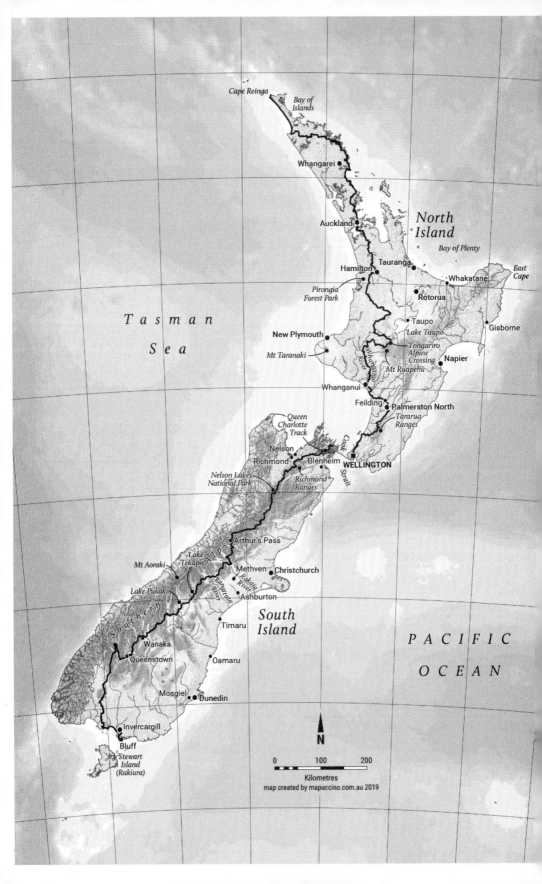

Kia tupato kia pai to hikoi
Me te titiro whanui, kia koa
Ki nga taonga kei mua i a koe

Walk the path in safety
Look deeply and learn
From your surroundings

Te Arikinui Dame Te Atairangikaahu, the Māori Queen
(23 July 1931 – 15 August 2006)
Written on a trailside plaque in the North Island

1

Freedom Walk

'I don't know if I can go on,' says Belle quietly, stopping in her tracks.

I wince. I've been dreading this moment, somehow sensing it might come. I think I felt it months before we even started. 'Really?'

Our boots sink into the soft sand, weighed down by the bloated backpacks strapped to our bodies. Above us the sun blazes from a blue sky cut with a thin trail of cloud, mirroring the frothy line of surf beneath.

'What do you think it is?' I ask.

'I have no idea.' She rubs a hand slowly across her hip with a grimace.

I can't see her face, hidden under a cap and oversized sunglasses, but the wavering voice is a giveaway. It's serious. I shift my weight and look down at my shiny new hiking poles disappearing into the sand.

We've only walked 18 kilometres. There's still another 3050 to go.

The faint call of seabirds floats on the breeze. Everything feels slightly distant, separate to me. Some autopilot mechanism has got me this far – to a beach in the middle of nowhere, with my life in a bag on my back – but now it, too, seems to have given up. *Now what?* My brain draws a blank, long since numbed. I wait for her to continue, stranded by my own emotional exhaustion and a feeling that the situation is out of my hands.

'Maybe I can hitch out from Te Paki Stream and head back to Kaitaia. See if I can find a doctor who might be able to work it out.'

Thoughts flash through my brain in the staccato of fireworks. *What is wrong exactly? Will it get better? What should I do?* Images from the guidebook come back to me – the dramatic and untamed wilderness ahead, all its inherent dangers. *I can't do this on my own.*

'You could keep going,' she says. 'You walk Ninety Mile Beach and I'll meet you at the other end. Hopefully I'll have this sorted by then and we can go on together from there.' Her face is blank, anaesthetised against emotion.

I lift my gaze to the empty beach stretching all the way to the horizon and beyond – 85 kilometres of sand all the way to Ahipara. I've never walked that far before. I've never camped alone either. At least the beach is a relatively easy stretch to start on. All I have to do is follow the coast. Even *I* can't get lost.

I yearn to walk, desperate to move after so many months of anticipation, but should I stick with her, give her moral support? At least she's offered me a choice. Can her injury be that bad? There was no fall, no awkward twist, no catastrophic moment, – just a limp that sprang up yesterday during our first three hours of trail. Surely that can be fixed. I just need to stay afloat for 100 kilometres, get this first leg done, then worry about what happens next once I get to Ahipara.

Beneath the disappointment the seed of another emotion starts to sprout: tiny but there all the same. Excitement? I'm surprised at myself. Whatever this obstacle is, I stand at the frontier of an adventure, with at least five months of unknown ahead of me. There's not another soul around, only the thousands of kilometres of space and wilderness that I've craved. I'm a tiny blot on a vast ribbon of sand holding a key to the potential for who knows what. Anything could happen.

It is the adventure I've been looking for.

I turn back to her.

'Yeah, okay. I'll do it.'

~

I asked for this. I wanted to be tested, expanded by a challenge that would let me see beyond where I was. I just didn't think it would start so soon. I'm not absolutely certain how I came to be attempting such an audacious journey anyway. The thread of an idea dangled itself in front of me a year ago and I pulled on it, and kept pulling, not really imagining that it could ever come to be, and yet here I am, on a beach, with a pack bulging with camping gear and a bundle of maps. I am, apparently, doing it.

The idea had begun in bed one night, while scanning the news section of a hiking magazine. The announcement rose from

the pages, a brand-new long-distance hiking trail. Te Araroa –
the long pathway, in local Māori language – a 3000-kilometre route
winding and rippling its way over mountains and forests, from
Cape Reinga at the northernmost tip of New Zealand's North
Island to Bluff at the southernmost point of the South Island.
A trail through a dynamic land formed by violent tectonic
plate collisions and geothermal explosions. Two long fingers of
rock and earth out in the middle of nowhere, exposed to the
churning weather systems of Antarctica and the vast Pacific
Ocean. A land that shifts and creaks and murmurs, sometimes
loudly, where earthquakes and volcanic eruptions are common.
A land unreasonably blessed with good looks and relatively
unburdened by the paltry five million people who live there.

New Zealand. I freaking love the country.

The announcement read like a proposal, slid across the table
before me. This one's for you, Laura. There wasn't a doubt in my
mind I should at least consider it.

I ordered the guidebook, and butterflies ruffled their wings
in my stomach as I flipped through images of snow-dusted
mountains, boulder-filled rivers and vast tracts of wilderness
without a path in sight. Kiwis are famously hardy. The fact that
the trail descriptions had been written by one made them all the
more intimidating. 'In places it's a hand over hand descent, but
without exposure in the mountaineering sense of hanging out
over a drop.' What did that mean exactly?

New Zealanders wear shorts in the middle of icy winters,
and a group of retired ladies mountain-biking for four hours on
a Sunday morning wouldn't raise an eyebrow. They invented

bungee jumping, the art of leaping off bridges with only a rubber band tied to your legs. New Zealand is the birthplace of Edmund Hillary, the first climber, along with Sherpa Tenzing Norgay, to summit Mount Everest. When a Kiwi says a piece of trail is not quite mountaineering you can be sure it's pretty damn close.

I downloaded the trail map for the section in question so I could worry about it in greater detail. The contour lines, whose parallel curves indicated changes in elevation, appeared as an almost solid block of brown. I couldn't imagine what it would look like in real life.

Firsthand accounts from the few who had completed it seemed to describe a trail that was raw and unpolished, made for proper adventurers familiar with forging across new territories. With morbid fascination I unearthed more and more things to be concerned about – the scores of unbridged rivers to cross, trackless tussock plains and exposed alpine passes – yet still I was pulled deeper into the idea, as though I were on some inevitable and unavoidable path, simultaneously scary and exciting.

I showed the book to friends and a work colleague scoffed at the idea, pointing out the first obvious hurdle. 'Yeah, right, what are you going to do? Just ask Ben for six months off?' *That's exactly what I'm going to do*, I plotted with a single-mindedness I didn't quite recognise. I knew it was a big ask – I was an executive assistant to a CEO, for God's sake – but I was going to ask it anyway.

I needed someone to come with me. There would be countless challenges ahead, countless opportunities to get lost. I would need someone to watch my back, to share the responsibility of making decisions and, possibly, the burden of having made a wrong one.

Belle agreed after a week of consideration and my stomach dropped into a new level of butterflies as the abstract concept of hiking the length of a country suddenly became a lot more real.

When I asked him, Ben, my boss, didn't bat an eyelid at the request. 'Sure, what do you need? Six months? A year?' He understood. This thing needed to happen.

There was the purchase of new hiking gear, visits to the physiotherapist to try to strengthen my dodgy knees, months of training. One by one the hurdles fell until nothing stood in the way of the journey that had to be done.

Adventure was the driver – the urge for one had been my companion for years, lingering, patiently waiting for me to be ready. A kind of knowledge that I was capable of more than I had done and that I should find out what that *more* was even if it scared me. What was possible? What would happen if I jumped out of my box? I needed a challenge to push me to my outer limits of being tired, dirty and mildly lost, but hopefully not so radical as to inadvertently kill me. Te Araroa sounded perfect.

Adventure may have been the lure but something else soon swamped it, like floodwaters rising. There is now a more pressing reason for escaping into the wilds. As I stand with Belle on the beach I feel the presence of another companion, an invisible one that had weaselled its way into my life over the last year and refused to let go.

I need to shake it off. I hope if I walk far enough I'll lose it. Lose it amongst the tangled forests, blustery peaks and empty beaches. Amongst the steaming volcanoes and tussock plains. Lose it somewhere along the 3000 kilometres ahead of me. I can't stop now.

~

Ninety Mile Beach: Freedom walk down the beach to Ahipara at your own speed, 80 kilometres, 3 days

'You've got the tent poles, I'll need those.' I poke through the gear we'd so carefully divided, now strewn all over the ground. A tangle of fat tyre tracks scours the sand around Te Paki Stream. It's one of the beach's few access points. A four-wheel drive or tourist bus should turn up sooner or later.

We eat lunch cross-legged on the sand, sitting ducks pounded by the midday sun. Emotion hangs heavy between us.

'Are you okay?' I venture.

'Yeah. Just disappointed.' Her voice sounds strained. 'I mean it's not a great start.'

'No.' I struggle for the right thing to say. Neither of us expected a road bump like this so soon. 'I'm sure you'll be able to fix it.'

'Yeah.'

The breeze blows hair in my mouth as I try to read the fluttering pages of trail descriptions I've printed. There's not much to know – basically there are 80 kilometres of sand ahead to tackle in any way I choose. A 'freedom walk', the notes call it.

We sit in silence, reluctant to part ways, but eventually I stand and brush the sand off my shorts. 'I should probably make a move.'

The tears spill down her cheeks as she wraps her arms around me and she feels tiny, like a fragile twig. I squeeze her gently then release her to hoist my pack.

'Well …' I turn to face her.

'See you later. Good luck. Look after yourself.'

'Thanks. It'll all work out.' I fiddle to slide my wrists through the loops on my poles and push forward in the sand. 'I'll see you in Ahipara!' I glance back over my shoulder with a wave. And then I head south.

~

Perhaps out of necessity, the simple act of walking changes my mindset in seconds, shifting from disappointment to the new goal of hiking the beach solo. With it the seed of excitement grows. Some part of me, deep inside, seems to be rising to the occasion, like a child that has been entrusted with a new responsibility.

Okay, Laura, you're going to walk 80 kilometres on your own, do you think you can do that?

Yes: the novice inside nods earnestly, although this same novice doesn't know what the hell she's talking about. What lies ahead? I've heard stories about this beach. Those who have gone before me speak about it in grim tones, complaining of sand that is too hard, too soft, of days of unchanging scenery that toyed with their minds. Many of them gave up their dreams to thru-hike the whole trail after walking it. I wonder how a beach can be so awful.

And what is beyond it? I have done day hikes in New Zealand before. I've seen its precipitous trails, felt the full force of its sudden icy winds. It's a wild place. No place for pussies. No place for someone like me.

Some might consider me adventurous but I'm not. I've jumped out of aeroplanes and cage-dived with great white sharks, but always I place my faith in others – the man strapped to me who will control the parachute and ease me gently to the ground; the metal cage robust enough to keep a toothy apex predator safely distant. It's when I need to rely on my own skill and judgement that things fall apart. That's when my imagination takes off like a freshly hooked fish running line off a reel. *What if x happens? What if I can't do it? What if I mess up?* I'm perfectly happy to leave my safety in someone else's hands, just not my own.

I know this attitude will not serve me well so I've been working on it, trying to rewrite the program of self-doubt that has always been there. I'm not sure exactly where it grew from, though there is no shortage of people in the world willing to share doubt and fear, no shortage of those ready to judge if you falter or fail. It makes trying all that much less appealing.

Barely a month before we left, Belle's husband declared bluntly, 'You guys can't walk that far. You've bitten off more than you can chew.'

My mum was doubtful too. 'Why not just do one island, or do it in sections? What about your knees?'

Even a complete stranger in the hostel, on the night before we left, felt compelled to write us off. He was tubby, American, greying at the temples. 'You're carrying all *that*?' he snorted as we sat on the floor surrounded by food and equipment. 'Ah, you'll *never* make it!' He shook his head and threw both hands in the air, dismissing us.

Curiously, I found almost as much discomfort in being around those who had complete faith in us. A friend mentioned me in the speeches at her engagement party, proudly announcing to the masses that I was embarking on an expedition to walk the length of New Zealand. A ripple of excitement ran through the crowd, accompanied by growing applause, while I sank nervously into my champagne. All I really wanted was to slink off quietly and give it a go, without any pressure. All I'd done, so far, was have an idea.

Then an old friend sent me an email. 'You're a fucking legend!' he wrote. 'I am so envious. You are doing something that screams out, "Laura Waters is not just a gorgeous babe but a fucking legend!" Go Laura, this is massive!'

I clutched on to his enthusiasm and trust in me with everything I had. His words helped me believe that I could do it and, despite the fact that I hadn't yet achieved anything, I decided to adopt them as my mantra. *I'm a fucking legend! I can do this!* Repeating those words seemed as good a way as any to try to brainwash myself into a state of confidence.

But now, as I walk the beach alone, nothing seems certain anymore. I push the dark thoughts aside. There have been too many of them lately. I *need* this. My mind and my body need it. *Just take it one step at a time, Laura.*

The beach rises gently on my left to a shallow lip lined with dusky green dune grass. I can't see beyond it. On my right, long ripples of surf roll lazily ashore from a vast and sparkling Tasman Sea. Ahead, the horizon is pure sand.

Okay, three or four days of this. I've got this.

I march with purpose, planting new hiking poles clumsily alongside my every step, trying to find the right rhythm. I feel like an imposter, trying to pass myself off as the professional hiker I will need to be to finish this trail. I feel a little rebellious too. Only Belle knows I am out here alone, and with her behind me only I will know my whereabouts from here on. I may well be forty-three years old but my mother would still definitely disapprove. Being under the radar feels strangely appealing.

I start to find a flow, my mind loosening its grip on thinking, letting attention wander. I notice the oystercatchers loitering at the shoreline, their spindly legs scissoring across the sand to avoid the advancing and receding waters. Birds cruise in wide, lazy circles against the glare of the sun. The waves whoosh and it's soothing, like something on a relaxation CD. My sister gave me one a few months ago, a three-part medley of ocean sounds, birds in a rainforest and rain with distant thunder. Did she know then how much I needed it?

The air here seems somehow different from home. There are new sounds – peaceful sounds that I haven't heard for a while – but overwhelmingly it's the lack of sound that's unusual. So much space, so much unfilled emptiness. At home there was barely an atom that wasn't vying for my attention.

The high-rise I work in perches at one end of a city whose

outer limits hold four million people. Streets heave, drivers lean on horns at congested intersections reeking of exhaust fumes. Peak-hour trains are jam-packed, oozing the stink of aftershave and body odour, humming with chatter, mobile phones and music leaked from headphones. Advertising is everywhere: at train stations, over hand-dryers in public bathrooms, plastered across the sides of trams, piped out over PA systems at petrol stations. You can't avoid it even if you want to. But here there is none of that.

I walk steadily for an hour or so.

I stop to take a few photos.

I walk another half an hour then drop my pack for a wee.

There is little to divert my mind from the task at hand. I feel it struggling with the sudden abundance of space and time, the lack of structure, like a newcomer at a meditation class constantly checking the clock.

I pull a map out and scan my surroundings but there's nothing in the way of landmarks with which to cross-reference my progress so I put it away again and keep walking.

Half an hour passes. I stop to munch a handful of nuts, taking my pack off to give my shoulders a rub, then realise I'm procrastinating.

Music! I remember the new earphones in my front pocket. I'd wrestled with whether to bring them, thinking perhaps I ought to just listen to the sounds of nature. Then I thought of the long walk ahead. There was no need to make it any harder.

I power up the ultimate 80s party mix – the good stuff, not the obvious, overplayed songs. They give my wandering mind an anchor and I feel a boost of energy, successfully squeezing another few hours of walking out of my body before my feet complain loudly enough to drown out the tunes. *Argh, come on!*

My boots have only been on one outing prior to this and they seem unforgivably rigid. I knew full well it wasn't a smart move. I should have worn them in ages ago but for months I found myself incapable of making a decision on which brand of boots to bring, or indeed whether hiking *shoes* might be a better option. Waterproof or non-waterproof? There were too many decisions to make, and too many things to learn. I watched the DVD on how to safely cross rivers then read half of *Wilderness Navigation* before the techniques got too complicated. The leaflet that came with my new GPS was a stupidly brief six pages that left me completely in the dark. Trawling the internet only raised more questions than answers so I gave up, finally paying someone else to load my route and show me the basics. The whole planning and preparation process drained me at a time when I had little headspace to spare. It was hard enough deciding what to eat for dinner let alone choosing the perfect kit to help me survive 3000 kilometres in the wild. Questions just rolled around in my head like tiny silver balls in a wooden puzzle, finding no escape. Still, I'm out here now and I feel better already. I breathe deeply in the salt air.

On the distant horizon great bruised clouds begin to gather. The beach's finish line is invisible. Where on this endless sand do I drop my pack and declare camp? How will I know when I've gone far enough?

Waikanae Stream decides for me, its sheltered dunes and fresh water all I need. I get pasta simmering in a titanium pot made for two and then think of Belle. What is she doing now? How is she going?

We met at a party eight years ago in Colorado, both of us working a ski season. 'Ooh, you're cute,' she said with a wink, squeezing my boob and flashing a smile full of perfect white teeth. I could think of no words to respond but I admired her fearlessness immediately.

We snowboarded the vast powdery slopes of Keystone and Breckenridge by day and drank gin and tonics on the town by night. Men flocked to her but she shooed them away and we talked, the stories of her wild life highlighting just how much I'd lived my own within the lines. Me, a woman who feels guilty taking a day off work even when properly ill, who is never late, always does as she's told, a woman who only ever fraternises with one man at a time. Belle, it seemed, was the opposite. Her boldness contrasted with my timidity, her confidence with my complete lack of it. But despite our differences we were bound by humour and some deeper essence of the soul that resisted definition – both of us wanting a life less ordinary, both of us searching for something.

Winter turned to spring and back in Australia Belle settled on the Gold Coast, surfing every day while I found a desk job amongst the corporate buildings of Melbourne, 1700 kilometres south. I envied her transient, carefree lifestyle but I couldn't complain. The job I'd landed was kind of cool – an executive role supporting a CEO in tourism and ski resort management. The CEO was cool. I even got a free ski-lift season pass. Ben took the time to teach me things, about strategy, business planning and feasibility studies, and I could sense the world of corporate opportunity stretching out before me like a banquet table, just waiting for me to dig in.

I could never have imagined then that eight years later Belle and I would be in New Zealand trying to walk 3000 kilometres. That she would agree to take six months out to come with me, even though she wasn't a seasoned hiker, the lure of the next crazy chapter in her life too great a temptation.

All logistical planning fell to me. At least I *had* actually hiked before. I sweated over spreadsheets, trying to bring order and clarity to all that needed to be done – trail research, gear selection, maps, trail notes, GPS coordinates, navigation and safety equipment, food, training – while Belle disappeared off the radar for months to surf some remote island in Indonesia.

A crackly phone call from some coconut outpost came through two months before departure. 'I got all your emails. How's things?'

'We've got heaps to do, Belle! I've made a start on the gear but you need to train too. This is big! When are you back?'

'Hey, chill, it's all good,' she said in a surfer's drawl. 'I dunno, I haven't booked my flight yet but I should be back in a few weeks or so and then I'll be on it full time. No drama.'

'They recommend doing a safe river-crossing course, plus we need to know navigation. Are you any good at navigation?'

'I'll just follow you. You're Boss Lady!'

A little part of me puffed with pride that she trusted me enough to lead our little party, while the vast majority wanted to yell, *Don't put your faith in me! I don't know what I'm doing!*

Five days on the Overland Track in Tasmania was my

biggest gig to date, a track with an actual track to follow. New Zealand wouldn't be like that. Long stretches of it are rated at the highest level, *Route standard: Suitable for people with above average fitness with high-level backcountry skills and experience, including navigation and survival skills. Complete self-sufficiency is required.* I doubted very much that I fell into that category and Belle certainly didn't.

I heard the change in her voice as soon as she returned to Australia – her tone more serious, a hint of concern at all that had to be done, a realisation of the magnitude of the challenge ahead. Departure day grew closer and I wondered if I'd sensed her enthusiasm dwindling just a little?

Alone on this beach, the uncertainty has returned. Did I unwittingly coerce her into doing something she wasn't truly prepared for? Was she ready to walk all day, every day, for months or was it my enthusiasm for *my* dream that sold her?

She's only gone to the doctor, Laura, let's not get carried away.

I always do this. Worry about stuff that hasn't even happened. Expect the worst. Disappointment just feels so familiar. I'm scared to want something so much only to have it whipped away from me. Better to keep a nice buffer of low expectations to cushion a possible fall.

I wander out of the dunes to the sea, the beach endless in both directions, the sky pink and hazy with sea spray. The scale of the emptiness is hard to grasp and only the birds share it with me. It seems so long since I've escaped into something so peaceful, so beautiful. I haven't felt like this in a while. Not in a long while.

~

Two geese gaggling over the pond stir me from my slumber and the pale dawn light filters into my tent, rousing me gently. I slept well.

Outside, yesterday's hot sun has been replaced by foreboding dark cloud. I collapse my tent quickly and tie my long hair into two blonde plaits. Yesterday they were tight, clean ropes, the result of Belle's handiwork, but today they are chunky loose knots, my first clumsy attempt at the style that is meant to stop the wind from turning my thick curls into instant dreadlocks.

Nothing's changed in the landscape yet the different weather casts a new light on it. Stiff winds send grains of sand swirling and bouncing to sting my legs. Small features grab my attention and in the absence of anything more dazzling they seem inordinately interesting: the body of a dead seabird half buried, one feathered wing reaching upwards like the arm of a drowning victim; a dead seal; big dark balls of seaweed heaped along the water's edge – shaggy monsters emerging from the sea. I hover over each feature, every find a small discovery, just for me.

When the clouds finally burst open in an unrelenting downpour there is nowhere to hide. Still, my new raincoat and pants are impervious to it. *Nice try, beach. It's going to take more than bad weather to stop me.*

Something catches my eye on the horizon, something that doesn't fit with the landscape, a red blob. I strain to define it as it grows, finally making out the shape of a car, dull and old, suspension bouncing over sand, and suddenly I feel alone, more alone than I did moments earlier. Exposed. Vulnerable. A 173-centimetre 'flag' drawing attention to itself on a flat, featureless beach.

The car draws closer, slowing its pace, turning to veer towards me. *What does he want?* I squint through the rain, body tightening. It pulls level and an arm reaches out from the driver's window. I stare at it, following it to a hand and then to the open tray of chocolate biscuits it holds, and my fears collapse like a house of cards.

Three young men inside lean towards the open window, grinning wordlessly but encouragingly – straining, it seems, to see what kind of girl would hike alone in the rain. The back seat is stuffed with camping gear and boxes of food. Travellers.

I pull a biscuit from the pack, give them the thumbs up. They nod and smile some more before easing forward to accelerate away.

You never know what you're going to get when it comes to people. They can be kind or creepy, as likely to offer a helping hand as to holler a wolf whistle, or worse. As a child, the simple act of walking up the street to the shops involved steeling myself against the inevitable jeering from the kids who loitered outside. Once I crossed the road to avoid them, but only once. *Why should I have to move?* I thought. Still, it was uncomfortable. A decade later a man approached me in a hardware store, flaccid penis pulled out between the zip of his faded blue jeans as he gazed, nonchalant, at the display lighting above. The man loitering in the bushes that lined the beach one childhood summer was scarier, the one who walked with purpose while holding his dick pointed at me like a gun. Every girl has had obscenities yelled at her from building sites or passing cars. As a fourteen year old on the walk home from school one day, a curly-haired blond in his twenties crawled the kerb next to me in his Kingswood. 'Where are you going?' he called, through the open passenger window. 'Do you want a lift?'

Humans can be weird, sometimes dangerous. But then some just want to give you chocolate biscuits. You never know which it will be.

The rain pelts with increased vigour, cascading water down my sleeves and onto my hands only to dribble slowly back up my forearms from the angle of my hiking poles.

An hour passes before I have company again, a huge sleek tour bus with darkened windows. It does a sweeping 360-degree loop in the sand and stops diagonally across my path, silently barring my way. With a hiss, the door opens, revealing the beaming face of a barefoot Māori . 'For energy!' He holds out a ham and salad roll wrapped in cling film.

'Thanks!'

Without pause he returns to the driver's seat, sealing the door behind him. I gaze up at the passenger windows, imagining dozens of tourists inside reclining on garish velour seats though I can see nothing through the dark tint. I suspect I look a pitiful figure but I would not trade places with them. The clean air and the rain on my skin make me feel alive.

I imagine the driver addressing his passengers. 'What you just saw there, ladies and gentlemen, was someone starting out on Te Araroa. She's going to walk three thousand kilometres all the way to Bluff in the South Island!' There would be coos of amazement from the crowd.

I power on for a few more hours, distracted by thoughts of my own heroism, until the cold seeps into my bones and my feet ache for a rest. A pause in the rain coincides with a rare flat patch of grass, and I pitch my tent and retreat inside. The bliss is almost instant. Warm, dry, horizontal and sucking on chocolate. My crumpled map shows the 26 kilometres gained, only four short of my longest day hike ever, just a few months ago. I hobbled for days afterwards. I don't feel too bad now, considering.

I lie staring at the rounded walls of my two-person tent, marvelling at its cosiness. Camping has come a long way since my first outing, as a child with my family. Back then we had a huge and heavy canvas 'house', complete with a kitchen–living area and two separate bedrooms divided by flimsy brown-and-orange swirly-print nylon – Mum and Dad on one side, me, my brother and sister on the other.

We favoured seaside areas. Somewhere we could paddle the canoe – modelled from fibreglass by my father – or rent a tinnie with a small outboard motor for fishing trips further afield, burning our bums on the aluminium bench seats in the hot sun. We never seemed to catch much but it didn't matter. It was about being together, eating picnics, watching the views pass by. We poked around in rock pools, played cricket, went on scenic drives at dusk, racing each other to be the first to spot a kangaroo or a wombat. And then at night we huddled around a card table, playing board games by the dim glow of a kerosene lamp. Everything we did we did together. We were a tribe back then.

My tent is much smaller now, a brown dome, yet still it's too big for just me. I wonder how Belle is going. Whether she's found a doctor yet. Whether she is cured.

The tent brightens and I crawl out to find the sun seeping through cracks in the dark cloud, spilling a warm, silvery glow across the horizon. Up and down the beach the view still hasn't changed – endless sand, dotted with seashells and sponges and dead puffer fish. I bet nothing much changes out here. It feels a grounding thought, an anchor of stability in what often seems an unstable world. I like this beach. I like it very much. Its subtlety, simplicity and space are its strengths. It has invited me to look harder for the interesting, allowed me to discover things gently, quietly, at my own pace. Plus I don't think I've ever walked a whole day on a beach before, let alone four. I'm enjoying it, if only for the simple experience of knowing what it's like.

Suddenly I feel compelled to fill the emptiness. I take off, running barefoot across the cold gritty sand with arms outstretched, swinging in circles, jumping, skipping. I whoop and holler, singing at the top of my lungs, releasing months of pent-up energy. I dance like no one is watching, because no one *is* watching. I release everything to the beach then float back to my tent to flop onto my sleeping bag, giddy with emotion. A few sobs of happiness escape my throat. I'm actually out here, doing the walk I have dreamed about for a year! After months and months of planning, I am in a tent, on Ninety Mile Beach, and it's just the beginning, the first of many months of adventure. If I feel like this after just a few days, how will I feel after five months?

~

Each day the tides creep along but I sleep in and, in a combination of narrowing beach and rising water, the firm sand I've taken for granted has gone. Rushing surf chases me five metres or more up the steep fringe of dunes, where the land dips and rolls: countless little undulations that sap my energy. I trip on half-buried grass roots and imagine I'm a lost explorer stumbling across a desert.

In the distant dunes I spy a huddle of small buildings. I slosh down the last of my water and make a concerted effort, reaching them just as the heavens unleash an ungodly amount of rain. There is no sign of life other than a small tortoiseshell cat wandering gracefully across the grass. It greets me like the unflappable host of a resort with no guests. *Utea Park, cabins available by koha*, says a sign. *Koha* – the Māori custom of giving a gift or donation. *Okay, cat, you twisted my arm.*

Thunder and lightning crack across the sky, and the wind and rain lash at my little cabin all evening, an invisible force pawing at me through the walls. Nature's moods are powerful, unpredictable and uncontrollable. I've always found the elements intimidating but in New Zealand the fear is justified. The country has a maritime climate. Nowhere is more than 100 kilometres from the sea, the generator of energy for wind and storms. The land's mountainous backbone rises suddenly from the Pacific Ocean to heights of nearly 4000 metres, catching rain and snow from the passing winds. The country is notorious for extreme conditions that can change at a moment's notice, regularly blindsiding those accustomed to more reliable weather patterns. Records are littered with stories of serious injuries – or even deaths – of unlucky hikers, even highly experienced ones, caught out by sudden changes in weather, flooded rivers, rockslides, or strong winds that blew them off precipitous bluffs. The challenge of hiking here lies not in venomous or man-eating animals but in the terrain and the elements themselves. I have prepared as much as I can for whatever we will face but the violence of the weather outside feels like a flexing of muscles, a reminder from Mother Nature that I will be at her mercy from here on in.

~

Morning arrives with a grey silence, the wet sand and grass beaten flat from an angry night. I march quickly, determined to make progress before high tide. On the distant horizon a battered white ute appears but random visitors no longer concern me. As it slows to a halt, the ruddy face of a man in his thirties leans out of the window.

'Hi! What are you up to?'

He's so eager I feel he could consume me with his gaze. I step back to make room as he opens the door, now standing very close in dirt-streaked jeans and a holey woollen jumper. They look like they haven't been washed in months.

'Well, I'm hiking the Te Araroa Trail –'

'So you're just walking the whole beach?' he cuts in.

'Yeah, and then I carry on south –'

'And so where do you sleep at night?'

'Oh, I just camp … along the beach.' I wave a hand vaguely into the distance, suddenly cagey about my night-time movements.

'Just in the dunes? On your own?'

'Yeah.'

He chatters excitedly about his farm nearby. 'Hey, you seem like a friendly girl. You can come and sleep at my place tonight if you want!'

His close proximity and keenness are unnerving. 'Oh, thanks. I'll probably just keep walking, though.' A silent voice whispers in my ear to put distance between us. 'I might try and make it to Ahipara tonight. I have a friend waiting for me.' I feel compelled to let him know that I'm not alone – well, not completely alone.

'Okay, well, if you change your mind.' He jumps back into the driver's seat. 'I'll probably see you around later.' With a spray of sand he's gone, accelerating north.

I walk briskly, ignoring the small blisters forming between my toes. If I can manage 31 kilometres today I could be feasting with Belle by dinnertime. It's a motivating prospect.

Hours later, the hum of an engine draws up behind me. 'So did you want to stay at my place tonight?'

'Thanks but I'm going to push on to Ahipara. I'm going to meet my friend there.' I say it decisively this time.

'Oh, okay. Well, nice meeting you.'

Swiftly he turns the vehicle around again and I'm glad I won't be camping alone tonight. It's Ahipara or bust.

The unwavering flatness gives my feet no respite. Over and over, they hit the ground in the same position with the same rubbing in the same places. Squished toes crowd one another's puffy, fluid-filled edges and my determined march fades to an awkward, flat-footed limp. Eventually Ahipara appears, a line of buildings on the horizon representing civilisation, rest and abundant food options. The final steps are torture. I wince, barefoot, across a stream lined with rippled sand that has bonded as hard as concrete, and then finally it is done – my first 100-kilometre hike, my first solo hike, my first stage of the TA.

Elated and exhausted, I sit at a picnic table to dust the sticky grains of sand from between my toes, reluctantly pulling my boots on again. Ahipara is tiny. Without a phone I can't call Belle to tell her I'm finished; that she can now come and collect me. I hobble the one main road, dazed and shell-shocked, looking for someone who can tell me where to go, how to get back to Kaitaia, 13 kilometres away, where she will be, in the same hostel we slept in before setting off.

I walk past a residential garage open to the street, overflowing with woodworking paraphernalia. A sign says *Gallery Open*. The smell of sawdust and wood shavings calls me back, tickling childhood memories of my dad spending hours in the shed, sawing, gluing and hammering lengths of pine into chests of drawers and wardrobes for our bedrooms. I would sit and watch him or sometimes have a go at the tools myself, hammering leftover scraps together to make something pointless like a spaceship control console. Dad was always good at teaching me stuff, at getting me to experiment, to question things.

I wander in for a closer look and see chunks of wood scattered around a workshop, spilling out onto the lawn in varying stages of completion.

'Hello!' A spritely old man lifts his head from behind a wood lathe. 'I was just going to have a cup of tea, do you want one?'

'Er, thank you.' I look down at my clothes, suddenly self-conscious. 'I'm a bit dirty …'

'Don't worry, just leave your pack out here.' He pulls the safety goggles from his face and I follow him inside.

Wooden bowls and plates scatter the tables, rims intricately carved or inlaid with the blue, green and silver swirls of paua shell. 'I use kauri,' he says, handing me a bowl, the wood rendered smooth as silk under his expert touch. Kauri trees are revered by the indigenous Māori , and are considered kings of the forest. Some live for more than two thousand years. Their massive girths and tall, straight trunks were too tempting for European settlers in the 1800s, who stripped the forests for construction. Once prolific in the North Island, these aged giants now remain in only a few pockets.

The man hands me a plate of juicy kiwi fruit while I try not to sully his cream sofa. I tell him about my hike, that I need to make my way back to the hostel in Kaitaia.

'I tell you what, I'll drive you over there,' he says chirpily.

Our meeting feels blessedly serendipitous. Maybe it was Dad's idea. He died three years ago, a sudden departure that occurred within the space of a day. I got the call at work. 'Your dad's in resus. Get here as soon as you can,' the nurse said. Then the line went dead. They tried for hours but the bleeding from his ruptured aortic aneurysm could not be contained. I hadn't visited him in two weeks.

The loss shook our family hard, a reminder, if any were needed, of the precious and precarious nature of life. That it needed to be lived *now* because you never knew when it might be taken from you. The suddenness of his departure was beyond tragic but we consoled ourselves with the thought that if he had to leave us then this was the best way, better than some long, drawn-out illness. He'd never have made a good sick person – he didn't have the patience for it.

2

A Dark Shadow

In the steamy embrace of the hostel's shower I feel like a million dollars, tired but uplifted, a sense of achievement coursing through my veins. Bathroom acoustics echo back songs sung with gusto. I dry off and stagger out with a towel around me to find Belle sitting cross-legged on the bed.

'You sound pretty happy,' she says.

'Hey! How's it going? Yeah, it was awesome!' There seems so much to tell her – the sand, the emptiness, the wildlife, the rain, the people I met. Words tumble from me and I find it hard to rein in my excitement.

'It's obvious you thrived out there.' She smiles faintly.

'So, what's the story at your end?' I sit down on the bed to face her, giving her my full attention.

'Well, I've seen a few doctors but no one seems to know what's wrong. It's only a small town.'

'Oh.'

'I need a physio or some kind of specialist.' She hugs her knees to her chest. 'I mean, I *want* to keep going but I tried to carry the pack again yesterday and straight away my hip hurt like crazy. It's like a sharp stab in the joint.' She pounds a clenched fist against her hip. 'I can't do this as it is.'

'Right.' I pause, wondering which bit exactly she can't do. Just the next leg, the next month – the whole walk? 'It's weird, eh. I mean you were fine before you left home. You were training on hills with a full pack and everything.'

'Actually, even when we walked to the supermarket the other day I could feel something, but it wasn't really bad until I put the pack on. Maybe I sat funny on the plane over here or something. I had that hip operation last year after that surfing injury. Maybe it's just flared up.'

'Yeah. Right.' *Please, surely it can't be over already?*

We sit in silence.

'You could still follow me by car until you feel stronger!' I feel like I'm clutching at straws.

'Yeah.' There's no enthusiasm in her voice, no energy in her body. 'Maybe I'll get a flight home and see my regular doctor. I looked into flights and they're pretty cheap. Then I can come back and join you on the trail later.'

She's already looked into going home? The thought of venturing on alone, beyond the relative ease of a straight beach devoid of navigational challenges, nibbles at my meagre confidence.

We sit quietly some more.

'Okay, but somehow we can still make this happen!' I eventually say. 'I'll keep hiking, you can come back and do day hikes with me if need be. A daypack would put much less strain on you. Just meet me on the trail and do sections until you're strong enough!'

'Yeah, yeah. We'll work something out.' She nods weakly.

We walk across the road to find dinner and my mood is lifted greatly by a juicy steak, fresh salad and hot apple pie. It's the reward I have been dreaming about all day. For a while we ignore the elephant in the room, laughing and exchanging tales of our four days apart. Wine magnifies the good vibes. The game isn't over. Somehow, some way, we will make it work – as a *team!* We vow it.

~

In the morning my feet hurt. Mysterious lumps the size of quail eggs have grown on the back of my heels and the balls of my feet are puffy. I'll have to do something about them.

We study my onward route over breakfast. The trail can be broken into rough sections determined by food resupply points – mostly small towns – that intersect the route, calling for anything from two to ten days of walking before the next shower and a chance to wash clothes. The section to come will take six days, stretching from west coast to east and finishing in the tiny town of Kerikeri. The map is tightly packed with contour lines, the trail notes promising thick forest with minimal signage and little water, and despite the success of my first stage I feel anxious all over again. Is it because I'll still be alone? Because I might get lost? A generic fear of the unknown? Or is it because this is the first of the hills, the first real test of my knees?

I didn't know it but I'd been walking badly all my life. My nan used to tell me I walked wrong when I was a kid. She didn't like the rubber thongs I wore on my feet. 'You're scrunching your toes up!' she said. 'You can't walk properly like that. You need proper shoes!' But every Aussie wears thongs. Anyway my problems turned out to be due to more than just footwear. While training for an ambitious Himalayan trek, ten years ago, the issue revealed itself in all its complicated and aching glory, an alarming twang under the kneecaps that soon accelerated to a pain so great I could barely negotiate a street kerb. A handful of physiotherapists confidently informed me I was using the wrong muscles when I walked and climbed, though I had trouble finding one who could explain to me how to use the right ones.

'No, use that one, not the other one,' said one, prodding me just above the interior of my knee. I stared blankly at the place she'd touched, wondering how on earth I was supposed to consciously decide which muscles I use when I move.

A cocky and unsympathetic surgeon suggested he could remove my kneecaps. 'That would stop the rubbing!' He sat back in his chair and regarded me with the air of a Very Clever Person who has solved a tricky problem.

I decided to keep my kneecaps, embarking instead on a long and frustrating journey of learning to awaken muscles I never knew I had. I learned to understand their interconnectivity, taught them to work together. I learned to engage my core and activate my butt, and discovered that if I did these things I would use the muscles in my inner thigh as well as outer, balancing the tension that pulled my kneecaps off line. Things got better – I started doing simple hikes without pain – but when Te Araroa appeared on the horizon I knew I needed to be bulletproof. For eight months I squatted, lunged and stretched my way through an intense strengthening program. I hope it's been enough. The training hike two weeks ago wasn't encouraging. Steep but only four hours in duration, it left me wallowing in ice packs for three days. I daren't dwell on it. I'm here now, I've just got to give it a go and get as far as I can. To help loosen any tight muscles I have decided to carry a thigh-width slice of physio foam roller, tied to the outside of my pack like a ridiculous bulky blue sausage.

I didn't get a chance to do anything about my shoulders. They're crap too. 'Multi-directionally unstable' is how one specialist described them. I've dislocated them so many times I've stopped counting. I last did it reaching for a handbag in the back seat of the car a year ago. My body has always felt flimsy to me, long and lanky with joints too flexible and muscles too feeble to hold it all together. I can bend my thumbs back ninety degrees at the first joint – and the second joint. It's as though my whole body might collapse at any moment like some push-puppet. I can only hope everything holds together for this journey, that my body does what it's supposed to do.

I carry our breakfast plates back to the kitchen as a young redhead walks in, clutching an armful of maps and a packet of chocolate biscuits. Long curls pile high on her head, revealing thick bone spirals threaded through her earlobes, and a dense mechanical pattern of tattoos covers one freckled arm like a sleeve. I strain for a closer look at her bundle and the maps look suspiciously like mine.

'Hi. Doing some hiking?' I nod towards her maps with what I hope looks like casual interest.

'Yeah, I'm walking the Te Araroa Trail. Or the "TA", as they say,' she says, smiling.

'Me too!'

'Are you doing it alone?' Her voice is soft and quiet, silky almost, with an American accent.

'Well, I was hiking it with a friend but she's got an injury she needs to sort out so I'm on my own for a bit.' *Please walk with me.*

'Wanna hike together?' she asks shyly.

'Yes! Great!'

'I'm Summer.'

She's young, maybe early twenties, a sculptor from Idaho on a mission to make one piece of art a day while hiking a whole country. A tower of river pebbles, an arrangement of wildflowers and animal skulls, or some artistic photography, perhaps. I think she must be super fit to attempt something so ambitious. It's intimidating but she seems friendly, sweet, despite the giant bolts and chain rings inked over her. The more she talks the more I sense uncertainty in her too and I wonder if she's just as keen for my company as I am for hers. 'Let's catch up later to make a plan,' she says and I walk away, clutching the lifeline I've been thrown.

I scribble a list of things to do before I can leave: order new, lighter, one-person tent, buy food, check email, upload photos, blog update, get massage, fix heels.

The local library has a computer but the internet connection is frustratingly slow. My throat starts to close just a little.

Breathe, Laura.

I wander the main street, catching my reflection in a shop window, surreptitiously checking my profile, smoothing down my t-shirt. *Does my stomach look a little flatter?* I straighten my posture, shoulders back. *Maybe.*

A pharmacist suggests a herbal cream for my heels. I book a half-hour massage. I'm tired. I just want to lie down and rest but there's more to do and the pressure of a deadline makes my head swim. I *must* be ready to leave with Summer.

Okay, the list, Laura, concentrate. Um, what was I thinking again …?

Neurons fire signals around my brain but, like old typewriter keys pressed at the same time, they jam ineffectively. My breathing becomes stilted; a fog seeps into my brain. I feel as though I'm trapped in a box slowly filling with water, the drowning inevitable and awful.

Where has that gloriously light feeling from the beach gone?

Panic starts to rise.

No, no, no!

~

The email landed in everyone's inbox. 'Ooh we're all in trouble now!' A cheeky voice called out from behind a computer.

A colleague passed me moments later. 'Hey, Laura, was that memo your idea?' The notification that told everyone to do their fair share of keeping the kitchen clean; that pointed out the dishwasher wouldn't empty itself.

The dig was said lightly, jokingly, but I rushed to the toilet and burst into tears anyway, letting them form a tiny pool on the marble laminate floor. There seemed to be no end to these tears, no reason required. Sometimes I cried from the sheer physical discomfort of the tension inside me.

I walked back to my office, closing the door behind me to try to create some protective cocoon, something to muffle the ringing phones and tapping of fingers on keyboards.

A colleague hovered outside, peering through the glass panel into my space and I pretended to be engrossed in the report in front of me. He wanted to ask me something but the barrier seemed enough to put him off and I was relieved when he walked away. I didn't want questions. My brain would struggle to answer them anyway. It had clattered to a halt long ago.

The tension had accumulated slowly and stealthily, almost without my knowing, until it became a monster beyond anything I knew how to control. For well over a year I had suffered it intensely although it was hard to say exactly when it began. Little moments of pain had scattered themselves throughout my weeks, my months, my years, interspersed with the occasional sharp stab of something much worse, and in not heeding the alarm I suddenly found myself immensely screwed.

The simplest, most intuitive thing to do had become the hardest – just to breathe. I felt the tension rise through my body. Like a thug on the street, it threw me against the wall, leaned heavily against my chest, wrapped its fingers around my throat and squeezed. It squeezed until I could breathe neither in nor out, stopping the ragged gasps of air that wanted to reach my oxygen-deprived lungs. I lived with the constant feeling that I couldn't quite fill them to capacity. My lungs actually *hurt*.

Noises hurt. The creak of the house as I lay in bed at night, the gentle drop of a toothbrush into its holder in another room –

my body flinched at every sound regardless of how slight, sending pain zinging across my skin from limb to limb. No matter how hard I tried to consciously command each muscle in my body to let go, they remained locked tight.

Sleep had been my only relief. In the midnight hours my body and brain escaped to another world, but come morning I had to head out into the real world again, into the city, into life, which twirled my brain around, so fast it couldn't keep up.

On the streets of Melbourne I tried to imagine the skyscrapers were actually the mountains of New Zealand, which would soon surround me. I willed myself to hang in there, but moment by moment the tension gathered and somewhere along the way I'd forget to breathe.

In my office, I looked around at the modular desk, with its two large computer screens and several tall piles of spiral-bound reports, the ones that months ago I'd confidently said I could analyse. I looked at the two telephones – one for switchboard, one for me – and I wanted to cry again, overwhelmed with helplessness. So low had I sunk that doing what I had always done quite effortlessly now seemed insurmountable. The small joys that kept office life bearable – a laugh with colleagues, cupcakes at a meeting, Friday drinks – were no longer able to keep me afloat. How could I make it through this day and then the next and the next? All I wanted was to be away, far away where everything was quiet, still, where no one wanted anything from me, where 'living' meant something that made me smile.

The air conditioning units, with an almost imperceptible hum, pumped out artificial air and I forced myself to breathe it.

I blocked one nostril with a finger to the side of my nose, inhaling deeply through the other, then swapped. Belle said it would help me breathe better. Another friend had given me some herbal pills. I don't know if she felt as bad as I did but she struggled at times too, as did Dave, who worked next to me, though he preferred yoga and meditation as a means to manage it.

Suddenly Jacinta from marketing flew past the glass panel in stilettos and a suit, looking for all the world like a woman who had her shit together, a woman achieving things, important things. She epitomised what we were there for. To *do* stuff. Do our best. Get paid. Work our way up. Get paid more.

The minutes dragged their sorry feet until five o'clock. I only had to walk one block from the office to the train station but every evening I ran the gauntlet. 'Have a free trial on us!' A perky blonde in shorts and trainers thrust a gym flyer against my stomach. 'We've got some great membership deals …' She kept talking but I kept walking, focused only on the traffic lights ahead.

Just got to get there, cross the road, get on the train, get home.

''Scuse me, can you spare a dollar?' A man slurred the words, reaching an arm up from where he sat amongst a grimy pile of cardboard. I pretended to be engrossed in my phone.

Three bounding youths in matching red t-shirts, carrying clipboards, scattered the footpath ahead. I scanned for the fastest line between them, clutched my handbag tightly, bowed my head and charged through. *Please don't talk to me.*

'Hi, how are you going? Did you know there are people in Africa now who can't get access to clean drinking water? For just ten dollars –' I hurried past as the tension in my chest ratcheted up a few levels. Dark suits, heels clicking on pavement: the sea of people swept me closer to the traffic lights. Even if I'd wanted to I would have found it hard to stop. My breath quickened but it was a shallow breath which didn't sate my lungs.

I need space! Please, everybody move aside!

I ducked and weaved through the crowded station, avoiding people, avoiding contact.

Gotta get on the train. Get home.

But, oh God, the train. Just the close proximity of others was enough to provoke a surge of cortisol. I felt exposed to their energy, an open bucket being flooded, weighed down by whatever was nearby. Dizziness poured into my brain, spreading through every cell, and in a growing panic I realised there was a distinct possibility I might pass out and fall off my seat into the crowded aisle. Soon I would give up on public transport altogether, instead walking the hour home to find more air, more space.

Home. Its location shifted over that year as I wandered in limbo. I lived in the home of strangers, house-sitting while they travelled to Europe for summer, then I lived in my mother's home. Before all of that, home was where the whole sorry mess first began.

I'd removed the problem from my life ten months earlier, removed the stimulus that had pushed me to this state, but the anxiety didn't stop and now I had this thing, this entity that had moved in and taken over my body, controlling my brain, my lungs, my heart, my limbs. Daily I reassured myself that the 'threat' had passed, the crisis over, that I could go back to being normal, but anxiety, it seemed, was unstoppable. There was no reasoning with it.

For over a year it followed me, from home to work, on weekends and holidays. And now it has followed me to New Zealand. If I can't shake it off here I'm not sure what I'll do.

3

Into the Forest

Herekino Forest Track: 15 kilometres, 8 hours
One of the largest groups of big kauri in the
north is about 2 hours in.

The track notes promise a long day. We leave early in Belle's hire car, winding back over the hills towards Ahipara, back to the trail where Summer and I haul our packs from the boot.

It's a tense goodbye, the air strained by unspoken fears and emotions. 'I feel like I'm missing out,' Belle sniffs tearfully.

'Well, it won't be for long. We're still a team!' I reassure her, but the words feel feeble to me. Tomorrow she will fly home. Does she really need to go? They have doctors here too. For a fleeting moment I wonder not *when* but *if* she will come back.

It's all good. Everything's fine. Keep going.

I leave her, following Summer up a road towards the forest, and within minutes the *click-clack* of hiking poles on tarmac resonates from behind. I glance back to see a man wearing the same pack as me. He's no ordinary day hiker.

'Hey, Mason,' Summer croons coyly. 'Mind if we walk with you?'

I turn to get a good look at him – tall and broad with a floppy cream hat covering a bald head. He slows his pace, eyeing us a little warily, with a faint smile. I sense a reluctance to commit to our team but, considering we are all headed in the same direction, his choices are limited.

'Okay,' he murmurs.

'We walked together for a bit on Ninety Mile Beach.' Summer fills me in as we fall in step.

'You're hiking the whole of Te Araroa too?' I call out to him.

'Yeah.'

Another one!

'Have you done much hiking?'

'I did the Bibbulmun Track a year ago in Western Australia. That was a thousand kilometres.'

'Wow, cool.'

A discreet sign points us into the Herekino Forest, which instantly envelops us in a dense cloak of green. The air is warm and steamy, thick with an earthy dampness. Silently we find our rhythm, climbing over the dark dirt that sprouts massive tree trunks – the famous kauri. They're even bigger than I expected. *How many people would it take to encircle one? Six, with arms outstretched? Eight?* I drop my poles to hold my arms flat against a trunk in a big hug, curious to see if I can feel anything emanating from such a giant, but it's hard to clear my mind with an audience watching on. With one cheek against its roughness, I gaze up at the thick, plate-sized pieces of bark lifting off – solid, unbendable, unbreakable, unlike any other bark I've felt before.

Muddy trails lead us deeper into the forest, up and down steep hills rutted with tree roots. Vines lay strewn across the ground like trip-wires, but despite the obstacles our pace is solid.

'You're a machine,' Summer puffs from behind.

I'm relieved our walking paces seem to be pretty evenly matched. Hiking suits my skill set. It took me a while to find my niche. At school, netball was huge – every girl played it. I don't know how they all seemed to know the rules before I'd even stood on the court; it seemed almost part of their DNA. Someone threw me the ball and I ran with it, wondering what the hell I should do next but by then everyone was already laughing. 'No, Laura, you don't run with the ball!'

Athletics was equally humiliating. The PE teacher set us an exercise – run on your toes and then run heel first, time yourself, and note which way is better. My time was faster on my heels. 'Wrong!' said Mr Black. 'Running on your toes is faster!' I was confused, not realising I could be wrong even when I was right.

It had taken me years to be able to 'run' in any sense of the word. I just couldn't get the timing right. I'd start out, concentrating hard – left foot, right foot, one, two, one, two – and by the time I got up to speed it had turned into a skip. If I ever had to get anywhere in a hurry I'd skip there. I was a damn fast skipper, though.

Endurance. Suck it up, push on. It's one of the few things I *can* do.

After eight hours we're still deep in the forest with no end in sight. I kick the leaf litter aside and shake out the groundsheet that marks my territory. Summer disappears into the forest with a trowel to sculpt some mud, and Mason retreats into his tent. Alone I cook dinner, gazing up at the immense greenness surrounding me. The forest seems dynamic, alive in a way that I find hard to put my finger on. Huge basket ferns sit in the crooks of tree branches high above. *What would they weigh? Twenty kilos? Perhaps even double that.*

I look at the map, calculating the 18 kilometres covered. It seems a piddling amount for the effort and sweat squeezed from us but perhaps time will be a greater indication of progress here than distance. Overall, 100 kilometres down and the next 120 kilometre section underway. So far I think I'm holding my own in the group. I don't *think* I'm slowing anyone down. At least for the next week I should be covered.

One step at a time. No point fretting too far ahead.

The wind wakes me regularly in the night, blasting the treetops in a noisy clatter. One ear stays alert for the sound of a basket fern breaking free from its anchorage and crashing through the trees. The full moon shines a white beam on the wall of my tent, silhouetting trees that dance on the flysheet like a shadow puppet show. Despite the intrusions I feel happy. For so long, it seems, I have cried myself to sleep.

~

It was around four years ago that I'd stood at that most significant fork in the road. A turning point where rather than turn I chose to push onwards.

I'd slunk out of his queen-size bed early, leaving the uncertainty in those soft sheets to escape to the rising sun, the soothing song of the dawn chorus. I left the bed where he lay to sit outside on the porch and think. Everything seemed so perfect – yet something wasn't.

Minutes later he found me, wrapping a warm, naked arm around my shoulders. For a while we sat in peaceful silence, both of us soaking up nature's brilliance. Then he said softly, 'What are you doing up?'

'Hey.' I leaned into him, swallowing the lump in my throat. 'I don't understand what's going on.' Was it six weeks we'd been dating? I searched for a way to say it without my thoughts sounding random and out of place, without sounding pathetic. How did one bring up such a topic? 'We should be doing it like rabbits at this stage.'

He laughed gently, pulling me tighter. 'Don't be silly. There's nothing wrong.'

His voice was so warm, so loving. I felt stupid, needy. And yet this wasn't how new relationships usually played out. Usually there would be a hunger, an insatiable desire, a need to explore and discover and connect. You'd find moments at any time of day or night, every entwinement revealing more of each other, perhaps binding bodies and souls a little tighter.

But not with Frank.

'Okay, got that done,' he'd mumbled to himself as he dressed after our last roll in the hay, as though I were a chore to cross off the to-do list.

Later in the day we went to a neighbour's barbecue.

Bowls of quinoa and kale salad, couples arm in arm, softly rubbing pregnant bellies and beaming at small toddlers playing. Domestic success.

'You guys look well!' said Peter from number thirty-two.

Frank wrapped a covetous arm around me and flashed one of his winning smiles, which made his eyes crinkle. 'Yeah, things are great, thanks, business is good! And I've got this gorgeous woman to keep me in line.' He pulled me tighter and planted a kiss on the side of my head.

I smiled too, trying to quieten the little voice inside that was sad. Perhaps I *was* just reading it all wrong, overreacting. He loved me. He must. He told everyone so.

But that little voice would not be quietened. It rang the alarm bell when he turned his back to me in bed, blaming a headache, tiredness, the height of the pillow or the heat of a summer's night. When he complained that sex took his energy away, as though he were some spiritual guru who needed to stay pure. He would do anything to avoid that most intimate of connections.

But connection was what I wanted, what I yearned for most. Love, honesty, acceptance. Someone with whom I could share all parts of me, the light and the dark, the good and the imperfect, someone with whom I could be real. I yearned for someone to be there for me, not to complete me but to complement me, a rock so that I might face life's challenges with confidence. I was tired of being strong, of looking after myself. I'd done it for so long.

~

We break free of the Herekino and I inhale as though bursting through the surface after a long free dive. Our boots crunch on the gravel back-country roads and we share stories of our lives. Summer grows vegetables at an organic farm. Mason drives forklifts. Our twenty-four hours together breeds a familiarity that would take months in the city, and the conversation quickly deepens. Mason's brought a book with him and its topics of consciousness and free will spark a lively debate.

'It's a choice,' he says. 'We're all in control of who we are.'

'To a point,' I agree, 'but you need to be aware. We're all doing the best we can with the knowledge we have but if you don't have awareness of anything different or better, you can't choose to *be* any different.'

'You can choose how you want to be,' he snaps. He doesn't exude the calm serenity of someone in control of his mind and destiny. I wonder if *this* is something he chooses.

'Are you happy, Mason?'

He exhales heavily, flustered and slightly annoyed, searching for words. 'Well … that's not a straightforward question.'

'Summer, are you happy?' I ask.

'Yes,' she answers softly, without hesitation.

'Are *you* happy?' He returns the question.

'I'm getting there,' I say.

Everyone's got a story. You can never tell just from looking at them exactly what it is but it's there all the same. I wonder what Mason's is.

~

In a settlement so indistinct it's almost a ghost town we search for water, finding a tap behind an old sports field. Another hiker has found it too, guzzling water in the shade, several more bottles scattered in the grass around him. He lifts his gaze, hidden behind orange reflective sunglasses and a floppy white hat, and in an American southern drawl introduces himself as Brad – another thru-hiker.

I can scarcely believe it. The trail is a relative virgin, walked by maybe 150 hikers in its lifetime at a push. I expected I'd be lucky to cross paths with anyone.

'I'm here with my buddy.' He gestures to a figure standing next to a petrol station across the road and when our water bottles are filled we walk over to join him.

'You guys hiking the TA too, eh?' Steve's Kiwi accent is immediately clear. Like mine but with the vowels shuffled around. He paces a little in the shade, as though unable to contain his energy, his voice rising and falling animatedly.

We continue on, a group of five. 'So you, Mason and Summer are hiking together, then?' Steve asks at my side.

'Oh, we just met on the trail actually.' I explain the story of how I came to be here, on my own, but not really on my own. 'And you guys?' I glance sideways at him, short brown hair tinged with rust, lightly freckled face. He's not obviously good-looking but there is something that catches my eye.

'Yeah, Brad and I have known each other for ages.' His accent turns *Brad* into *Bread*. 'We both did the Baekdu-Daegan across Korea. That was seven hundred and thirty-five kilometres. Brad has done the Appalachian Trail too. I've been working over in Korea for years, anyway, thought I'd come back home and do this one. Walk my own country!'

The Appalachian Trail – a 3500-kilometre slog down the east of the USA, top to bottom. A little warning flag waves in the dark recesses of my mind: Summer and I are the only ones with no pedigree in distance.

We camp in a farmer's field on the edge of the Raetea Forest. After dinner I find Steve and Brad lying out under an indigo sky with a rising moon, blues music filtering quietly from the small tinny speaker between them. 'Pull up a seat.' Steve shuffles up, offering me one end of his sleeping mat. I perch on it in the darkness, arms wrapped around my knees, listening to the banter and jokes. It's been a while since they've seen each other but a long history of escapades has clearly forged a strong bond. I laugh at their gentle digging and humour, immediately comfortable. Steve shifts position, causing my end of the mat to bounce slightly, and it's surprisingly thrilling to be connected by the air beneath us. Just to be close to a man again.

There's a faint flutter of feathers and I notice a small owl on a branch, silhouetted by moonlight. 'Look!' I gasp, pointing.

'It's a morepork!' Steve exclaims. The bird tilts its head sideways to peer down at us.

I've never shared a moment with an owl before. It's exhilarating. Watching it with new friends, I decide it's a good omen. This second stage will be okay.

~

Dense bush – infrequently maintained,
markers not reliable

Steve and Brad's tents still hum with faint snoring. We leave them to sleep in, knowing our shared path will connect us again. Mason, Summer and I set out into the Raetea Forest with the kind of innocent enthusiasm born of a good night's sleep combined with ignorance of what lies ahead. Dark tree trunks reach high into a canopy we can't see for all of the ferns and shrubs at their base. Sinewy vines trail over logs; spiderwebs catch tiny golden leaves that have fallen from above. Species fight for space and every surface is either covered in moss or festooned with fine ferns so laden with moisture I am sure I could get a cup of water just by squeezing a handful of them in my fist.

Giant leaves rustle heavily against each other as we bash our way through a path so overgrown it's barely visible. It feels more Rwandan jungle than Kiwi forest and I half-expect to come across a family of mountain gorillas hiding amongst it. Glutinous mud clings to my feet; the hills are persistent and vicious. I watch Summer negotiate a steep descent, stretching a leg out dead straight in search of lower ground. She wobbles backwards and forwards, sliding, clutching at ferns lining the track. Kiwis call this 'tramping' and it suddenly seems a far more apt description than hiking. *Tramp – to tread heavily, trample, trudge.* In time each of us falls over in the mud – on our bums, our sides, our knees.

The way starts to close in even more. I haven't seen an orange triangle in a while. Are we even going the right way? 'Hey, Mase,' I yell, 'can you see a marker?' Summer and I pause in the thickness, listening to the distant crack of branches and the sound of foliage being thrashed around.

'Yeah, this way!' A voice filters back.

The forest is an obstacle course. Hours and hours of snagging vines and giant fallen logs that we must crawl over with a loaded pack or under on hands and knees in the mud. Its relentlessness starts to break me, daring me to release the tears gathering behind my eyelids.

At four we down packs for our second quick break of the day but there is nowhere to sit that isn't overgrown or muddy so we just stand there, shovelling chocolate and nuts into our mouths by the handful, the exercise purely a refuel. Intellectually I know the forest is neither for us nor against us but it truly feels like it is conspiring to keep us there, *wanting* to trip us up, to wind its creeping tendrils around us and keep us forevermore.

When the sun is low in the sky the route starts to look recognisable again as a path of passage – wider, flatter, the mud replaced with short grass. We power along in a swift march until we're finally released onto an open plain.

The Raetea held us captive for eleven hours. The morning's camp seems so long ago it might have been another day.

~

The next morning brings road walking that punishes my body in a different way – hours of unchanging flat ground pounding my heels. I try to take my mind somewhere else and then wonder if it's possible to consciously switch off pain receptors.

At Apple Dam we camp in a small grassy clearing near a pool of water so choked with reeds it is impossible to get anywhere near it. By dinnertime five other tents have squeezed in alongside us. I watch one party arrive after another – first Steve and Brad, then Rita and Martin, a pair from Germany planning to hike only a section of the trail. A tall figure clad entirely in khaki emerges from a small tent next to mine and I introduce myself.

'Ah, we've already met. In Kaitaia,' he says quietly with a shy smile. 'Liam.' He nods hello.

Have we? Stubbled face, short dark hair, full lips, angular glasses. I take in his features and search my memory, finding a partial match from a scene in the hostel kitchen. *Did he have longer hair then, perhaps?*

'Oh,' I say smiling sheepishly. 'Hi.'

Next to the water tank I meet Antoine from Paris, a tall beanpole with blue eyes and cropped grey hair. He's rinsing his one blue t-shirt under the tap. 'Allo!' His smile seems to spread well beyond his face. 'I meet Liam on the bus to the start of the trail. Now we walk together!' He beams proudly.

I can't believe I have found so many other TA hikers. I join in with the laughter and chat, but inside my body hurts. My feet throb, my back and shoulder muscles are wringing tight, and my glutes are so knotted they hurt just lying down. But it's not just physical. The emotional energy it takes to keep pushing on is draining too. Can I keep doing this day after day for months? My knees have so far behaved themselves but the overall stress on my body seems to have no end. It's hard to imagine I might ever get used to it.

I don't for one moment consider giving up but it does cross my mind that I might have a miserable five months ahead of me.

~

The trail along the Waipapa River is so overgrown and washed away the notes recommend walking up the riverbed itself if conditions allow. I'm all for it. I'm sick of these half-baked trails. I surrender the instinct to stay dry, allowing the water to gush into my boots, feeling its silky coolness wrap around my thighs, and in that moment I feel like a kid again – before it mattered whether my shoes were wet or dry.

The river is the only clear passage through the dense greenery, a magical pathway lit by beams of sunlight, the fragrant air humming with birdsong and the flit of blue kingfishers. For hours I wade through thigh-deep water, from one raised pebble bank to another, before returning to the dirt for a long climb.

I'm too busy hiking to be anxious. The nonstop exercise forces me to breathe deep, the air too clean and rich in oxygen to refuse. I'm so engrossed in surviving the moment that I can't think about the past, or dwell on those countless little moments that slowly drained the life force from me. I'm too distant from the bombardment of the city to feel buried under its weight.

The land's beauty lifts my soul while its nature crushes my body, and by the time our ten-hour day is done Summer and I hobble into camp like the walking wounded.

But the others are disturbingly chirpy. I watch them wander in one by one. 'Great walk today, eh!' Steve powers in with large strides. Then Antoine, pacing briskly as though he just popped out to the shops rather than walking 25 kilometres through rivers and up and down steep forest. Maybe he's charged by the French Foreign Legion marching music he listens to. I watch him casually sling the pack from his shoulders to the ground, manhandling it like a daypack. Somehow he still looks immaculate, brown scarf lightly knotted around his neck, not a bead of sweat on his face or a hair out of place. Should I even be here? Maybe I've been ambitious, naive, to even consider such a trail without having stretched my legs beyond 65 kilometres.

~

Follow the markers and watch out for the farm animals.
(Note: move gently, never put animals in a corner or separate
mother and offspring; when going through a herd of heifers
or steers, be steadfast but wary as they are excitable.)

Just one more day of walking separates me from a bed, a shower and a day of rest. The thought is like a beacon and I cling to it, heading east over rolling green fields fringed with daisies, over stiles, dodging black and white cows and electric fences. The distant Bay of Islands, shimmering in blue, heralds our arrival on the east coast and the notion of progress nudges me onward, keeping me focused on the one goal in my steadily wilting brain – to reach Kerikeri and rip my boots off. I never imagined my feet could hurt so much. Perhaps you don't actually ever break these boots in – they break *you*.

I follow the scattered line of hikers in front of me blindly, like a caterpillar in a chain. Architect-designed houses start to appear amongst vast manicured lawns. Oh, to lie on the soft sofas that must be inside! An artificial scent wafts on the breeze – the smell of clean people. They round the bend, a couple in white cotton pants and pressed shirts, pushing a cloud of deodorant and perfume that seems shockingly foreign.

Finally it is over. In the hot shower of a cabin park I stand dazed, easing knots out of my matted curls and processing the thought of having put another 120 kilometres behind me. I tease the clumps apart with my fingers and yank the comb through, impatient to finish the job and lie down, then I notice the pair of huge, swollen feet on the tiles beneath me. I gasp, unable to recognise them as my own.

Guilt courses through me: I've pushed my body through such hardship. *It'll get better soon*, I promise. At least I hope it will. I mean, people do this. There must be some trick to it that I just haven't worked out yet, some method that will make it all bearable.

~

I check my emails and discover one from Belle. She's been sick with a cold and hasn't yet seen a doctor about her hip.

Hasn't been to the doctor yet. I mull over her message with a mix of worry and annoyance. She's been home five days and hasn't been to the doctor because of a *cold*? She's suspended our big adventure, kept its future hanging in the balance, because of a sniffle, a sore throat?

'But I have convinced my mate Alan to come over with me,' she continues. 'We're going to rent a car and follow you and I can hike with you for bits.'

She sounds bright, a photo attached of her and her friend grinning next to a computer, working on logistics. It looks convincing. She's still committed.

Silently I plead with her to hurry. I think about the mountains ahead, the unbridged rivers, the long paddle on white water that's an official part of the trail. I think about all the things I cannot do alone. I have company now but I can't bank on it continuing. These people have their own plans and I was never part of them. Maybe they'll walk faster than me or skip bits, or maybe they'll get sick of my company. There is no one just for me, no one who will stick by my side regardless of whether I'm slow or injured or need a rest. There is no one who cares whether I'm tired or struggling, no one who gives a toss about my whiney little fears. I need the other half of my team.

~

Our rest day coincides with the town's annual street party. The roads are closed to traffic in the evening, cars replaced by dozens of food and wine stalls and stages pumping out live music. After the body's trauma, all is quickly forgiven and I am happy again. Clean, rested, hopeful. Steve buys me sauvignon blanc in a plastic glass. The slab of beer he shared with Brad back at the cabin has made him even more animated. He owns his space, confident, cracking jokes. He's funny, though Brad's funnier. But Steve's Kiwi accent alone is enough to make me smile.

Alcohol slips into my veins, a tingling anticipation at what the night might bring. For the first time in many years I am single and without a scrap of adult responsibility. I forgot what it feels like, to have no mortgage, no job, no bills, nothing to think about other than being here. It's as though I am twenty-six again, when I used to cruise the dance floor of the beach pub at Barwon Heads with my friend, scanning for the cutest surfers we could find. When it felt the world was at my feet.

My body is older now, my hair not as blonde, but I feel just as much potential, just as much lightness. Steve bounds around, laughing and chatting to others. Easy, relaxed, fun – how things *should* be. It's been a while.

'We're now one-fifteenth of the way there!' Antoine shouts over the masses.

It sounds more manageable than thinking about the 2850 kilometres still to go. We raise our plastic glasses to celebrate.

I sample another wine from a different vineyard and then join the queue for a chocolate crepe but it's long and the Frenchman tending the hotplate lavishes an artisan's attention on each swirl of batter. My desire for one is almost a physical ache but I stop torturing myself and head back to the quicker wine queue.

Good music, new friends. I move through the crowd chatting to people I know and people I don't. Suddenly Steve is beside me, lacing his fingers through mine and leading me through the melee to dance. The crowd corrals us closer together. He slides an arm loosely around my waist and then lets it drop as though it were just a casual touch, but all the while his eyes bore into mine.

I am drawn to him. Alcohol and endorphins have taken over. The rest of our crew are somewhere not far behind, perhaps watching. I hold back.

The music stops and someone with a microphone announces the evening is over. A collective groan rises from the masses but there is no one more disappointed than me. Bodies disperse, leaving Steve and me looking at each other through alcohol-glazed eyes. He tilts his head to one side. 'Do you want to go get a drink?' I smile and nod.

But then the rest of our group is there, swarming around, sweeping us back to the cabins. The moment is lost.

~

Beginnings are always a thrill. A touch is electrifying and one person's voice can sound like the most beautiful thing ever heard. We fill in the gaps of what we are yet to know, extrapolating a future perfection to match the current bliss. Beginnings bring all the excitement of hopeful possibility without the complications of reality.

That's how it happened with Frank.

Things were good in those very early beginnings and that good start propelled me a long way. It gave me something to look back on and hope to revive. He swept me off my feet, showering me in an almost overwhelming display of love. There were flowers plucked from the garden and artfully arranged in bouquets, dinners cooked, hints of a long future together.

He was tall and I liked that. A six-foot, two-inch frame that was cosy and safe to nestle into. I liked his short blonde hair, his muscled forearms and soft deep voice. I liked that he nourished his body with good food and gave it plenty of exercise. I liked the Converse trainers he habitually wore, whether at home on weekends or at work in the design studio, and his navy convertible: not as a trophy but as an experience. Riding in it was just plain fun.

I admired him for his creativity. When he wasn't designing houses at work he was creating at home, fiddling with some complicated computer software to make electronic music. It wasn't my scene but he looked cute, holed up in the spare room under a pair of chunky headphones, body pulsing to some silent beat.

We talked for hours, marvelling at everything we had in common − a love of nature, of adventure, a desire to shirk the city in favour of the countryside. Perhaps we could buy a house in Tasmania, somewhere surrounded by mountains and ocean. Grow our own fruit and vegies. Drink rainwater. Live off the grid.

He made dinner one night, roast lamb and red wine by candlelight. 'I love to see a woman with a good appetite!' he said, smiling as I tucked in, thrilled to find a man who didn't expect women to survive on a diet of salads and self-loathing.

I liked his friends, his family. Every puzzle piece fitted perfectly. I was happy.

Except for work.

I lacked a passion, a purpose. I loathed the restriction of doing the same job every day, of travelling to the same place, of being confined by four walls while the sun shone outside. 'Why don't you quit and I'll take care of you?' Frank offered. I never dreamed of taking him up on it but the mere fact he suggested it warmed me. I felt treasured, cared for.

He made wild announcements, phoning my sister to tell her how much he loved me. While out with my mum he grabbed the bill, grinning and saying, 'I have to get a coffee for my future mother-in-law.' It seemed crazy but I didn't care, I just lapped it up, our courtship blooming like some romantic movie montage.

Then one afternoon we walked hand in hand through a park. A young girl crossed our path, perhaps in her early teens, t-shirt pulled tight over a tummy bulging gently over her waistline.

'She needs to lose some weight,' Frank muttered.

The needle on the record suddenly scratched off its groove.

I looked at him. 'Fair go. She's probably only about twelve.'

'It's not healthy, she's fat.'

'She's not fat!' I looked at her again. A little rounded, maybe, but certainly nothing to worry about. She was still growing, still finding herself.

Later he pinched an inch of his own stomach, skinny with a hint of washboard, and grumbled that he needed to do something about it. 'What are you *talking* about?' I said. 'You've got a great body! Geez, I hope you don't judge me the same way!'

'No, no, of course not.' He laughed lightly, brushing it off.

We'd been together three months when my fortieth birthday arrived. Choked with emotion, he presented me with a gift – a wad of cash to spend as I pleased, accompanied by a handmade card. He lay on the bed, watching me open it, lips pressed tight to control the wobble that had surfaced, eyes blinking back tears. He looked vulnerable. Distressed.

We didn't have sex on my birthday. That made me sad. I was forty and I wasn't getting laid; it didn't seem right.

~

Exactly four years later, the day starts brighter.

'Happy birthday, Laura!' They are the first words I hear, floating over to me from the direction of Steve's tent. Even in the early hours he sounds impressively chirpy. It's been three days since the street party that left me with buzz.

'Thanks,' I yell back, stretching out in my sleeping bag. 'Happy birthday, Brad!' I call out again. His mumbled reply drifts back to me, entwined in a yawn. Tucked in his pack is a bottle of whiskey. Our birthdays will be shared.

I eat breakfast, gazing out to sea, happily watching a little black schnauzer bounding across the sand. Steve sneaks up from behind, surprising me with a present of three muesli bars wrapped in a piece of paper with a birthday message scrawled on it. I'm touched at the gesture. Carrying food for three days only to give it to me. Some girls want diamonds, I'm happy with muesli bars.

Last year Frank gave me nothing. 'I'll take you out for the day,' he cooed. 'I'm so busy, but I'll give you my time. That's my language of love to you,' he said, head tilted to one side in faux sincerity. By then I was beyond caring. If suffering my company for a day was his idea of love then I didn't want it. In the end he didn't even give me that.

It feels weird to be attracted to someone again. Since Frank there's only been one brief liaison, with a porn addict named Benny. He was nice enough, I guess, though we never really got off the ground. 'Your boobs are kind of small,' he said one day in a tone you might use to broach a sensitive subject, like body odour. *Yeah, well, your dick's kind of small but we make do,* I said. Well, I said it in my head, anyway. But Steve seems really decent. Happy. Thoughtful. Nice.

The group makes a staggered departure and I leave with Mason for 20 kilometres of steeply undulating forest. A sharp pulling sensation starts gnawing at the muscles of my right thigh. I've never felt it before. It's not the usual pain of fatigue. It feels weird, worrying.

The day is hot, the patchy forest doing little to shelter me from the sun's rays. Sweat drips from my nose and eyelashes and the pain in my leg becomes like a knife stabbed deep into the fibres of my inner thigh, twisting viciously with every step. It takes my breath away.

The hills are relentless, the worst terrain I could encounter under the circumstances. False summits are a tease. I repurpose my hiking poles as crutches and rack my brain to work out the cause. *Am I not walking right? Have I let my posture slacken? Is it because I'm carrying extra weight?*

I splurged on a pair of hiking shoes in Kerikeri, unable to bear the boots anymore where the terrain might allow me to get away with runners. My feet are much happier for it but now I have a heavy pair of boots dangling awkwardly from my load.

I tune in to my body, scanning each muscle group, searching for clues. I think my glutes have stopped working. I direct my attention to them, willing the muscles to reactivate, but they refuse, leaving my thighs to do all the work. I hobble on, blinking back tears, alone with the pain even though Mason is only a few paces ahead. Today of all days – another crap birthday.

By the time I reach the tiny coastal settlement of Whananaki I can barely get my body up the two steps to the modest campground. I grab armfuls of ice cream, Cheezels and chocolate from the general store, intending to blow my pain away with dopamine, but instead the sudden influx of sugar leaves me unsettled, nauseous and anxious, my head pounding with a dehydration headache.

A handful of hikers unite in the camp. Rita and Martin give me a block of chocolate as a present and I remind myself that I'm not alone even though I feel that way. Soon they will leave the trail to travel elsewhere. Already we have lost Summer to shin splints and missing toenails. There is nothing stable about the company I keep.

I wander to the estuary, hoping that the sunset might be soothing, and then glimpse, on the far shore, barely visible, two tiny figures hiking into the distance. *Steve and Brad.* My heart sinks further.

Between us spans the Whananaki Footbridge, the longest of its kind in the Southern Hemisphere. I walk only a fraction of its 400 metres, trying to breathe as deeply as I can, urging my chest to relax. It's awful. I feel almost 'Melbourne-anxious' again. Silently I beg some higher help for relief – anything to ease the choking tightness around my throat and lungs. And what of this pain in my thigh? If I can't even manage a few steps now without my pack, how will I be able to continue tomorrow with it? I don't want to lose my group but there is no question that if my leg doesn't make a miraculous recovery I won't be going anywhere.

I escape into the night, limping to the furthest boundaries of the camp to a fence line, and try to keep my tears as quiet as possible. From the darkness a horse wanders towards me, silently placing its head next to mine. There is no nuzzling for food, no movement, just a big warm head pressed gently against my cheek. We stay like that for a long time.

~

I found a note from Frank, scrawled on a scrap of paper, tucked into my handbag when I went to leave for work one day. 'Love you so much. Can't wait to get naked and wrap myself around you tonight.' I smiled at the effort. He was trying.

Eighteen months we'd lived together. It was a big mistake. If I'd had an alternative when my lease expired eight months after we met it never would have happened, but I didn't and so I'd found my life bound even further to this man, despite the red flags that had waved ever more vigorously as time passed. I yearned for the independence that living apart once gave me, to make the possibility of leaving infinitely simpler. So I could call it off in an instant without having to endure a campaign of earnest promises that I wanted to believe while I packed up my life once more. Instead I felt trapped, with no way out other than to dream that each promise, each crumb of hope, might come to something.

That afternoon, I sat on the back porch with a chilled wine in hand as the sun slipped behind the purple wisteria in our yard. Magpies warbled into the air and studied the lawn for worms. It wasn't a big garden but it was ours, a pocket of peace in an otherwise manic life. Work was done, the ninety-minute commute behind me. I inhaled the scent of tree oils and waited.

Finally, there was the sound of the garage door opening, his footfalls to the back of the house. Then he was there.

I turned to give him my best smile, keen to pick up the baton he'd passed with his note, eager to fix the relationship and make it work again. 'Hello!'

'Hi.' He squeezed out a tight smile, dropped his satchel to the ground and kissed me on the cheek.

'How was your day?' I pulled out the deck chair beside me, beckoning him to sit. He dropped into it, eyes boring into the wood of the table. He took a deep breath, renewed the grave look on his face and my heart sank. I knew the script.

'*What* a day. The traffic was awful. It took me over an hour to get home.'

'Oh well, you're home now.' I squeezed his hand.

'*You* couldn't do it.' He scowled.

A half-laugh escaped me. 'Are we competing?'

He leaned in suddenly, wincing at something on my chin, one hand at the ready. 'You've got a hair …' I held still while he tried to pluck it between two fingernails.

'Don't worry about it, I'll get it with the tweezers later.' I wanted to move on, to share a drink, get back on track.

'My forearm is killing me. It's using that damn mouse all the time. Look …' He held his right arm up in front of me, turning it around as though I might be able to see the tension.

I pulled it to me and rubbed my thumbs up and down it, kneading. 'Have a rest. Do you want a glass?' I nodded at my own.

'No.' His sigh was heavy, almost theatrical. 'I *have* to do a workout. I *need* to.'

'Just get a drink and sit down for a minute first.'

He disappeared indoors and I heard a bloodcurdling scream from the kitchen that stopped my heart. I leapt up and ran inside. I found him lying on the floor, one foot raised against the benchtop, arms flailing over his face. I rushed over, fearing the worst, looking for blood, looking for bones out of place. 'What's wrong?'

'Argh.' He breathed the words through gritted teeth. 'Stubbed my toe. On the fridge.'

I stood up, stepped back. Looked at him lying on the floor.

'I think it's okay now.' He blinked quickly, licking his lips, glancing at me sideways. 'It really hurt, though.'

I walked away without a word.

Drama. I first witnessed it weeks after we hooked up – a slice of bread caught in the grille of a toaster. He'd thrown both hands up in the air, eyes like saucers, and stepped back to glare at the appliance, daring it almost to release his bread. He never simply shivered, he got 'mild hypothermia'. Fear of fainting from low blood sugars would have him throwing himself to the ground pre-emptively, as though chased by gunfire. Usually I tried to soothe, to reassure, but he looked ridiculous lying on the ground like that and I told him so. I never heard another word about low blood sugar.

Early evening passed with him smacking a punching bag in the garage while I sat alone on the porch. We ate dinner. He disappeared to the spare room with his headphones and his computer and the sadness crept over me like a blanket of fog. Why didn't he want to spend time with me? What was wrong with *me*?

I lay in bed waiting, knowing that he wouldn't come back until it was late, until I was nearly asleep. How long had it been? Months at least. The last time had been awful. I'd sat astride him – my partner of two years, a man with a look on his face that could only be described as thinly veiled panic. I remember his eyes locked onto mine with intense focus, mouth tight in determination. He let his eyes wander tentatively from my face down my body – looking, but not wanting to look. Much as I might look if a huntsman spider crept across the curtain rail. I looked down, following his gaze to my breasts, my stomach, then back to his face. I didn't know what to say. There was no point continuing.

4

Finding My Feet

Somewhere in the midnight hours a miracle occurs and by the morning I can walk again, perhaps due to anti-inflammatory drugs or simply rest. Regardless, by day's end our group has disbanded. I told Mason not to wait for me. I didn't want to hold him back. Besides, we were all headed to Ngunguru so I was happy to walk by myself and catch up with them all there. But the small seaside town has no clear camping, and by the time we reach it our group scatters and I find myself alone.

I do know where to find at least one friend, though. I pull out a phone number from my pack: Mary, a friend of a friend from home. She welcomes me literally with open arms, graciously ignoring the stench of dirt and stale sweat, and then runs a hot bubble bath. 'I made you a birthday cake!' she calls out as I sink into the water, feeling ten times happier than I did on my actual birthday. 'There are some packages here for you too!'

My new one-person tent has arrived along with some edible birthday gifts from home.

At dusk I wander the main street to search for my crew and find only Mason, stretched out in a motel room. He tells me he's moving on the next day. There is no offer to leave together.

I head back to Mary's to check my emails and discover one from Belle.

> *My dear friend, I am writing to let you know that at this point I cannot continue with the hike.*

Waves of heat and cold ripple from my face to my feet and back again.

> *Since arriving home I have spent only two days out of bed. My hip has been the least of my worries.*

I scan the text quickly. It's long, detailing an array of problems. Dizziness. Weakness. Some virus from Indonesia. Her body, she feels, does not want to be under the pressure of the hike.

> *For now I have to leave you with the epic journey ahead. I know you have it in you and I am so happy for you that you had the strength to go on solo. You are following your dreams, your joy, and you are living in the moment. You are so much stronger than you think you are. I hope that this trek meets all your expectations and that you love your time in the wilderness.*
> *Love Belle*

Chemicals flood my body in a churning wash and it takes a while for my brain to become coherent again.

I sit back in the chair.

Well, that's that then. Now I am well and truly on my own.

Fuck.

~

I need a rest day. I need to regroup. I head out to buy a mobile phone – Belle had the only phone we'd planned to carry between us – and post my two-person tent home. Then I seal the seams on my new one-person tent and review the notes for the trail ahead. I've already walked 335 kilometres. The current has caught me. I must at least try to continue.

I'm annoyed though not surprised. Perhaps I should have more compassion for whatever it is Belle is going through, but all my suspicions about the depth of her resolve have come rushing back. My own effort and commitment to this mission were never matched and this announcement, genuine though it may be, feels like the final, gutting failure to honour a pledge we made nine months ago.

Far beneath the anger is resignation. Some tiny cell deep within was waiting for this, expecting to face it alone. It seems to be my path, a situation that has recurred throughout my life. I recall the time a boyfriend had to pull the pin on a diving holiday days before departure after slicing his foot open on broken glass. He was okay but there was no way the wound could be allowed to get wet, so our plans were shot. With leave from work already booked, I decided to travel elsewhere solo. A few years before that, a work relocation meant I had to drive 4000 kilometres from Melbourne to Cairns. It couldn't be helped but it was a long trip to do on my own. I'm not sure if it's fate willing me to be on my own or simply that in the face of being alone I push on anyway. Some people might prefer to pull the pin but if you wait for others to be ready to come with you, you can wait a long time.

In my thirties I planned a three-month tour through South America but within a month of departure the tour company cancelled my trip. Not enough people wanted to do it. I'd pondered the options with my mum, poring over alternative tour brochures, looking for dates that would fit my flights, but no one else was running in low season. I could either travel independently or cancel the trip altogether.

'What a shame.' Mum was crestfallen.

I took a deep breath and ran a hand across the back of my neck, over and over, trying to coax a solution from my head.

'Have you got a sore neck?' she asked, suddenly concerned.

'No, I'm just rubbing it.'

She paused, thinking. 'Why don't you see if Pete can go with you?'

'I think he's in Europe at the moment.' An old family friend, Pete was always travelling somewhere.

'Well, you can't go on your own.' It was a statement, plain and simple.

I imagined jostling for position on long, crowded bus journeys in a land whose language I didn't understand. Pickpockets, strange food and no one there to look out for me. And yet why not? Why *couldn't* I go on my own? Plenty of people did. The thought of it scared me but it was better than not going at all so I went, a journey that challenged and rewarded in equal measure.

Now, again, the goalposts have moved, leaving me with no real alternative.

You're already here, Laura. Just give it a go, see how far you get.

I look at my maps. The next few days don't look especially challenging though it's hard to be sure. I've already been caught out more than once. Overgrown paths or no paths, minimal or non-existent trail markers. Sometimes it all seems very straightforward but just when I'm lulled into a sense of security, and following a fairly well defined path, I realise I should have deviated on some minor overgrown one much earlier.

I dig out the few phone numbers I've accumulated and find Steve's. I type out a message.

In Ngunguru and heading south tomorrow. Was sorry to have missed you the other night. Anyway, keep in touch.

Within minutes the phone beeps back.

Me too. Brad was keen to camp further on. What's your plan?

I fill him in on the latest development and he tells me they are no more than 15 kilometres south.

We'll be walking from tomorrow afternoon. Keep in touch and if it works out, walk with us to Auckland!

I feel boosted, not just at the promise of company but at the thought of seeing Steve again. I re-read his words, trying to determine just how sorry he was to miss me.

I need to catch them.

~

*Firmer sand can be found away from
the mangroves… A white marker indicates
where the most shallow crossing has been
found to date.*

Mary sees me off early, packing me off with the remainder of my birthday cake to share with 'all my friends'. It's delicious but weighs a tonne. And I don't know who I'm going to share it with.

I feel a surge of positivity in the morning sun, recharged after two nights of rest and Mary's wholesome food. And I have clarity. No more wondering if or when Belle might return. Now I know exactly what I'm dealing with, and this fact alone seems to free up some energy.

The estuary crossing 34 kilometres away is best done at low tide, at around 5.30pm. I power-walk forest and coast, and when I reach it Antoine and Liam are there, reclining on the grass in their underwear to escape the afternoon heat. Their familiar faces lift my spirits greatly. I offload some cake, mentally calculating the weight reduction in my pack as they tuck into large chunks of it, and then we sit in the shade and talk while the water drains out to sea.

Antoine flits from one topic to another – work, aircraft, rugby, travel. At thirty-five years of age, he's divorced with grey hair. Life is busy in Paris, he says, too busy. He feels expectation there, has trouble saying no. This hike is a temporary liberation from it all.

Liam works in insurance in the centre of Brussels, though he doesn't like it. He's tired of conference calls and corporate life.

He speaks quietly, unhurried, the words falling from his mouth in their own good time. He says only what needs to be said, not wasting excess words on anything frivolous. His presence is a calming influence.

They seem an odd couple yet all three of us have at least one thing in common – we're all escaping *something*.

The crossing is two kilometres of knee-deep water, sand and mud. Antoine takes a photo of me sinking ankle deep in the gloop. 'No, no, over there.' He waves a hand to the right. 'The mud is deeper there.' He giggles cheekily.

By the time we search out a campsite on the other side I have walked 40 kilometres, a seemingly ridiculous distance. It's a new personal best.

~

A muffled beep escapes from under my pillow. A text from Steve: *We were invited to stay in a farmer's house last night, just after the estuary.*

I pack up and embark on the remote expanse of Ocean Beach with Liam and Antoine, unsure if Steve and Brad are behind or ahead of us. The three of us spread out in search of our own discoveries. I find an albatross laid out in the sparkling wet sand, wings spread, looking serene in death. Antoine dashes from one side of the beach to the other like a bumblebee, investigating a dead penguin or a piece of driftwood. Liam strides calmly but purposefully, bundled up in khaki pants and a long khaki shirt with a matching floppy hat that reminds me of Doctor Livingstone. He's tucked his pants inside his socks to defend against the blowing sand, and fingerless gloves shield his hands from the sun.

But I welcome everything the beach wants to give me with a broad smile. I embrace it! The sun on my skin, the salty breeze in my hair, the rush of the ocean in my ears. I feel the vitality and energy of it, its purity, its aliveness.

From a cliff top we spy two tiny figures walking the beach and I recognise the blue t-shirt and floppy white hat, and the long strides of a man next to him in brown. Brad and Steve. Maybe Liam and Antoine would be happy to walk with me, maybe not. I wouldn't want to risk pushing it. I've never wanted anyone to be with me unless they really wanted to. Rejection is a pain too great to bear.

At school I was always the last to be picked for sports teams. What kind of sick teacher makes their pupils select their own team members one by one, anyway? One by one, in order of ability or popularity, until there is no one left but me and 'the fat kid'.

On a youth camp, too, I fell foul of this selection process. We were in a bleak forest, in the rain, in a draughty old canvas tent not quite big enough for the eight of us allocated to sleep in it. It was decided that one of us would have to move to another tent and the camp leaders organised a silent ballot, handing out pieces of paper to each child on which to write a name, a name of someone they thought should be the one to move. I'd barely known these kids hours, hardly said a word; I was the one who moved.

Shyness never helped. It's the gift that keeps giving, a self-perpetuating feedback loop of awkwardness leading to exclusion, leading to more awkwardness. I'm sure I must have missed social cues, said the wrong things. I felt as though everyone was in on information I was not privy to. Too shy to elevate myself, I opted to isolate instead. Maybe it was all in my head but, somehow, not being wanted started to feel normal.

Decades later I met a friend who was able to bond with every person she encountered. She did it effortlessly – an easy smile, always laughing. I really admired her for it. No doubt it was her openness that connected us so tightly in the first place. One day she confided, 'You know those people you go to hug sometimes and it's just like' – she squirmed, screwing her face up – 'awkward?'

'Yes!' I recognised the type immediately. 'I'm one of them!'

I've definitely improved over the years, started to feel more at home in the world. My face no longer turns red when people speak to me. Yet still the early hardwiring is difficult to break.

But now I've been officially invited to join a team. Steve has deemed it so. I am sorted for the next 200 kilometres. I feel like a circus acrobat swinging from one pair of outstretched arms to the next. Safe again.

Bream Head lifts all five of us above the treetops. Nearby, a towering plug of volcanic rock protrudes from thick forest while a smattering of rocky islands float like distant ghosts on the hazy sea. We descend to a beach, plunging into the water to wash away the day's sweat and dust.

I drape my body over a rock to dry. Eyes closed, I let myself drift.

Waves rush gently at the shore.

Somewhere in the trees, birds tweet melodic and clear.

How does a little bird make such a pure, strong sound, I wonder, a sound so much bigger than its maker? I let one eye crack open slightly and see the green forest tumbling steeply to the sand. I become aware of everything – the heat from the rock beneath me, the breeze brushing my face. It's essential. Magical almost. The rock is like a physician's bed and I feel nature working on me, filling in pieces that have crumbled away over the years. Parts of me are coming back, parts I forgot about. I'm being made whole again.

Somewhere along the way I lost myself. Actually I don't ever remember *being* myself. It seems for years I have simply existed – well travelled, productive, but searching for that space where I felt genuinely me. I hung out in bars, saw bands, went shopping, attended festivals, did everything everyone else did, but there remained an unfilled hole deep in my being, waiting to be satisfied.

Frank's entrance into my life illustrates just how lost I was. He never should have been part of it. The stinging pain of those bleak times seems a world away now, here. How did I allow it to get that bad?

I remember he found me in the shower one morning, crying.

'This is not normal, Frank!'

'Everything's fine,' he murmured soothingly. 'I was just really tired last night.'

Everything was *not* fine. I knew it. I wished he would either change or admit it and let me leave. Somehow his admission of the problem would reassure me that I was reading the situation correctly. That I wasn't going mad. That I was right. I needed his agreement to free me of my indecision.

'We don't kiss. You never want to have sex.' I looked down at my body, the small mound of my stomach, my boobs limp in the shower's heat, and felt a wave of uncertainty and self-loathing. There must be something terribly wrong with me if my own boyfriend couldn't bear to touch me.

'That's all behind us now,' he spoke quietly, soothingly.

Behind us.

The revelation months earlier – that I wasn't the first girlfriend to be held at arm's length – had given me hope. He conceded that maybe he did have things to deal with after all, things inside that got in the way of us. He said he would seek help, that he was committed to us. Everyone's got a story. I didn't understand exactly what his was but I wanted to support him through it, to help him move beyond it, so we could get on with our lives.

The water seemed to weigh me down, its steam suddenly suffocating.

'I *love* you,' he cooed through fogged glass, pausing before adding encouragingly, 'I've actually been quite attracted to you lately!'

Actually.

Quite.

The two words cut me to my core. My legs wanted to collapse beneath me while my arms wanted to swing a baseball bat at him.

Did he even know what love was? Did *I*? What was I doing here?

I screamed, I cried.

And then I stayed.

~

When the daytrippers have gone I put my tent up. Steve lounges on a sleeping mat down the beach, plucking grass seeds from a new pair of socks, long and striped red and green. 'Only sixty cents from the second-hand shop!' he yells across to me, beaming. He looks like a Christmas elf. Still sexy, though. I watch him out of the corner of my eye – broad shoulders, sleeves pulled up tightly against thick forearms.

Behind him Antoine wanders in search of a place for his tent, pacing the beach's fringe with a furrowed brow. He unfurls his sleeping mat and lays it out, moving it from spot to spot. He lies on his back, hands clasped across his chest for whole minutes at a time, testing out plots of land, eventually finding one that pleases; then he begins grooming it, brushing aside twigs and stones until a perfectly smooth oblong remains. I must be either lazy or too tired to care, I think, lying back on my lumpy, sloping site.

We do not see the sunset, its ball of fire disappearing over a horizon far away on the west coast. Instead the sky turns a warm pink, purple then blue. The stars rise and I brush my teeth, casting a glance down the beach.

Antoine's tent has moved. It mustn't have been such a good site after all.

~

The next day Liam and Antoine break trail for a rest but I push on with Steve and Brad.

We walk barely twenty minutes before Brad drops his pack on the grass and sits cross-legged next to it. 'If you're going to walk with us there is something you should know.' He pauses while he pulls a small plastic container from his pack with a clay pipe inside. 'We're gonna get stoned and steal all your stuff.'

'Right.'

'You want some?'

'Nah,' I say, screwing up my face. 'But thanks. I might keep moving.'

'No worries, Laura, we'll catch you up in a bit!' says Steve.

I walk on, feeling disappointed, all my daydreams about Steve coming to a crashing halt. I hate that stuff.

Later, in the pink dusk, we camp amongst sand dunes.

'Want some music, bro?' Brad pulls a tiny speaker from his pack.

'For sure. How 'bout some Creedence?'

Our handwashed underwear hangs side by side on a log to dry, my nylon hipsters with lace trim, one pair of stretch boxers and another loose cotton – all of them black. We have no secrets now. Brad pokes his simmering noodles with a pair of chopsticks, Steve does a few yoga stretches, and all the while the gentle banter bounces back and forth. Brad has a dig at Steve about his increasingly bushy mop of hair. 'Well, the ladies don't seem to mind!' Steve grins with mock swagger.

They're trying to give up cigarettes, using the hike to begin anew. Marijuana doesn't count.

Sounds of the ocean float across the dunes, the shifting colours of sunset giving way to a black sky filled with a sweep of twinkling stars. Creedence rocks quietly. The night air starts to bring a chill to the body and again the small plastic container comes out, mingling ocean-fresh air with the sickly sweet smell.

It took me a while to work out what made me so upset about my ex smoking dope. Not the last ex, the one about three before him. He tried to hide it from me but you could always smell it. It brought on a rage that spewed forth from me suddenly, surprising me as much as it did him, later followed by a deep sadness. I think it was the fact that he, or at least his mind, went to another place, a place I had no desire to go to, and in going there he left me on my own. I still don't like the smell of it.

~

A low rumble of farts disturbs the morning quiet, interspersed with audible snuffling and stretching. I sit in the doorway of my tent, eating breakfast, as a head pokes through a zip opposite, already donned in floppy white hat and orange-mirrored sunglasses. Brad staggers out with a yawn, stumbling into his sandals and nearly tripping over the edge of his tent in the process. It makes me smile. I've been awake for ages.

Early starts are rare in my new team unless there is a low tide beach walk to be had. Sometimes they saunter with all the time in the world, chatting about current affairs and the meaning of life while I wait ahead; other times they suddenly double the pace, leaving me chasing after them. The only constant is the morning 'toot', usually early in the day when a suitably discreet and scenic location has been found.

Steve is friendly – complimentary but not flirtatious. It seems odd if we both like each other that nothing should happen but I don't push it. Maybe he's not that interested after all. Maybe he doesn't think *I'm* interested.

For days we meander the east coast, dipping from sea to forest and back again. The trail is dubious at times and navigational clues dwindle, leaving us wondering. The advice given by maps, signage and trail notes diverges and we must use skill and intuition instead to find the route. I turn the map around and then around again, trying to orient it, trying to match it up with what I see around me, but the trail notes sound cryptic without collaboration from my surroundings.

Brad takes control, relying on a freakish internal compass that I envy deeply. It's tempting to surrender the whole task of navigation to him but I still want to decide the way for myself, to think it through and know that I could find my way if I needed to. What decisions would I make if they were not there and would they be the right ones?

I'm grateful for their company though at times I feel like an outsider. Each night Brad pulls out his speaker and we huddle, listening to podcasts or bluegrass. It's not my favourite music but 'Cumberland Gap' is all right. They drink whiskey. They fart. A lot. Brad lets out a roller so long it's as though he's trying to see how far he can stretch it. He stares at me blankly the whole time, watching my face contort with mild disgust. One raised eyebrow accompanies the final flourish, a little extra burst, then, 'Oops.'

I wonder if he's trying to tell me something, that perhaps he'd prefer a boys' team. It's hard to read through his deadpan manner if he's cool with me joining them or not.

Torrential rain entices us to dry out for a day in Matakana, a peaceful town on the edge of a river by the same name. I treat myself to a huge breakfast at a cafe on the waterfront and flick through the weekend paper, finding a page on fashion in the lifestyle section that features a montage of 'must-have essentials'. *The perfect pair of white pants? Hardly essential.* Every day we have led a simple life, our only responsibility to find our way, find water, food, somewhere to camp. They are my essentials.

I flick to the arts pages, my favourite, a section that usually brings comfort, knowledge, perhaps inspiration, but it too seems disappointingly unsatisfying. It's as though I'm seeing it with different eyes. I *kind* of enjoy it but a much larger part of me finds it to be just noise. There are reviews and discussions, opinions declaring what is good and what is not. It seems unnecessary, just stuff clogging up my brain.

I abandon the paper and watch the ducks instead, pushing at the water with webbed feet, picking at foliage with their beaks and nudging pink, purple and yellow flowers aside. A gentle breeze skims the water, sweeping their feathered bodies along the surface. It makes me smile.

~

Warning: Forestry & farming operations …
take a left down another track heading
southwards to an old logging landing
with its remnants of waste logs.

As we draw closer to Auckland the pace picks up. Steve has plans to catch up with family and somehow a deadline has been created around something obscure like an international cricket match to be watched with friends. To keep up with them I have to move fast. I power-walk. Sometimes I even jog a few paces. Steve does his best to bridge the gap between me and our speedy navigator but I start to tire, feeling more than ever like the third wheel.

Two days out from Auckland we camp in the bleak wasteland of a logged forest. Wind gusts across the open land, violently shaking my little tent, and I lie inside feeling the tightness in my chest and throat return. What lies ahead? Beyond Auckland I will finally forge ahead solo. For better or worse.

The city rises from the landscape like a behemoth, growing with every kilometre, the largest and most populated in the country with 1.4 million people. I pick my way through the Sunday crowd on the North Shore beaches. Bodies lie scattered over the silken sand in bikinis and board shorts, smelling of sunscreen and perfume, while mud from the Dome Forest still cakes the bottom of my pants. Stunning houses line the coast and I entertain myself by wondering which one I would choose if I had a few lazy million lying around.

Finally the iconic spire of the Auckland Sky Tower comes into view and it dawns on me the progress I've made. I am 596 kilometres into my journey, a distance far beyond anything I've walked before. There have been long days and aches and pains, but overall I have found it more than manageable. My body no longer screams out for mercy on a daily basis, my 'cankles' have subsided and the heel pain has nearly gone, although a curious numbness in my big toes remains. Somehow I've managed to get this far without really having to face the frightening prospect of walking alone, and on the whole I'm starting to think that if I just keep going one day at a time then maybe, just maybe, I can do this.

Steve and Brad escort me to my hostel and our goodbye feels awkward. When will I see them again? *Will* I see them again?

'Thanks for letting me walk with you.' My gratitude is heartfelt.

Steve waves it off. 'Nah, you're awesome.'

Brad echoes him.

We hug and they disappear, swallowed by the bodies walking the city streets.

I spoil myself with a single room, the hostel equivalent of a penthouse suite, on the top floor with wraparound city views. I dive onto the king-size bed feeling the thickness of its white sheets, savouring the thought of having a home for the next four nights.

Showering takes ages, delicious hot water steaming the grime from my pores. Afterwards I study my reflection in the mirror over the sink. It's been more than a month since I've had a good look at it. The sun has bleached my hair and left a golden t-shirt tan on my arms. I stand on tiptoe to see more of my nakedness and wonder what Frank had seen that was so awful. It was true I would never be a Victoria's Secret model but I could hardly be considered overweight. Regardless, I deserved love anyway, didn't I? Yet he couldn't even bring himself to touch me. Sometimes he even visibly shuddered. 'Well, my mate Gary says he struggles a bit with his girlfriend's body too,' he justified.

'She just produced a child for him!' I retorted.

It's obvious now that we shouldn't have lasted beyond a month but back then it wasn't so clear-cut. And the more I ignored my gut the more unsure I became. Maybe he had a point. Maybe I *was* fat, ugly, annoying. I'd always been aerobically fit but maybe I should have done more sit-ups like he wanted, worn a full face of makeup every day, spent more money on fashionable clothes. Maybe I should have gone to the gym daily instead of just three times a week. After a while it seemed difficult to know what was reasonable.

People have said stuff before – the portly dive-shop guy who gleefully pointed out a crease in my belly as I sat on a kayak. The friend who poked my stomach above my jeans with a smirk, saying I had a bit of a muffin top. It wasn't *much* of a muffin top. Certainly nothing like his, anyway.

But those girls in the magazines didn't help things, nor did the ones on TV commercials, prancing about on beaches, sipping soda in skimpy bikinis with sun-bleached locks. Compared with them I had a lot of failings. It was so hard to separate truth from myth. Just what *should* I look like?

Through Frank's eyes I learned to loathe myself more than ever. I saw the new grey hairs, the wrinkles, the wobble under my upper arms. It's annoying. I never used to give my body a second thought. I accepted it as it was, grateful for what it did for me, but now I find myself analysing it, searching for imperfections just as Frank did. I want to be free of it.

Exhausted, I flick off the light switch and stretch out.

Time passes.

Ambient light from the city probes my eyelids. There's a persistent low-level drumming from the air conditioning, its vibration permeating my entire body. I can feel my body objecting to these invasions. It's become used to the soft sounds of nature, the rush of water, the swish of wind in the trees.

I try to block out the noise, scrunching the sheets over my ears. It doesn't work.

~

In the morning I starfish on the bed while the hosts of a TV breakfast show buzz about Christmas. It's only a few weeks away and the conversation revolves around what presents to buy for whom, how to entertain the hordes, how to juggle the many social engagements and avoid stress. None of it applies to me. The tips on how to stay trim during the festive season are so far off my radar it isn't funny. I can eat whatever I want these days and still I lose weight.

Their chatter seems loud, hectic, overwhelming. It suddenly strikes me that every solution they offer is in response to a problem we ourselves have created. How odd, I think. Why would we do that? Create stress and then seek tips on how to avoid it.

With Belle at Cape Reinga, the northernmost point of New Zealand and the start of the Te Araroa trail. My fears about embarking on this five-month odyssey were tempered a little by the fact I had a companion to walk with.

Four days of sand on Ninety Mile Beach. Not long after taking this photo, Belle had to leave the walk with a foot injury. It was only the beginning, and suddenly I was completely alone.

Dodging vines in the Hunua Forest, just hours before getting completely lost.

A dazzling sunset from camp on Mt Pirongia.

There's more to New Zealand than green forests and snow-capped mountains. Walking the volca desert of Tongariro was a whole other experience.

Paddling the Whanganui River for six days, an official part of the trail.

After falling over twice in one morning it was a relief to call it a day at Waitewaewae Hut, in the Tararuas.

ew Zealand has plenty of swing bridges. Thankfully this one was relatively sturdy.

Heading through a valley towards the Waiau Pass. There's nowhere to go but up and over.

Celebrations after finishing the North Island. It was so heartening to discover the friendship and camaraderie that can develop between a group of strangers on the same trail. (L to R Antoine, me, Dieter, Isabel, Joe and Liz.)

Much of the Richmond Ranges is rugge and exposed, making for tough walking.

The Nelson Lakes National Park is one of my favourite sections of the trail, despite my trepidation: not long before I tackled this section, an experienced British hiker had perished after falling off a cliff and landing in a glacial lake 180 metres below.

Home for the night after my first day hiking completely alone in the South Island.

Camp before crossing the Rangitata River which shimmers in the distance. I had to hide from a testy bull who begrudgingly shared his patch of grass with me.

The Rangitata River is around three kilometres across and a major hazard zone as water levels can change quickly.

Afternoon at Crooked Spur Hut.

Morning at Crooked Spur Hut. When the snow set in, I was glad of my decision to delay pushing on over the next pass.

Happily descending Stag Saddle in the sun after three nights snowed in at Royal Hut.

Camping on the shore of Lake Puk with Mt Aoraki in the distance.

One happy hiker at Martin's Hut, the last of the trail. After five months of walking I was stronger – inside and out – than I'd ever expected.

My life has been reduced to eating, walking, sleeping. All the fat has been trimmed off it, all the unnecessary accompaniments that complicate things.

I turn my attention to the maps and trail notes scattered around me on the bed, trying to work out my next move, to guess how far I can go in a day based on the terrain, the possible camping opportunities and food resupply points. I feel nervous, wondering if I will be able to find my way okay, wondering where I'll camp, whether I'll be safe.

I flip from notes to maps and back again. It seems to take an inordinate amount of brainpower to process and I am simultaneously amused and dismayed at my struggle to assimilate the information and come up with a plan.

It's difficult to know if anxiety has permanently fried my brain or whether I am just crap at this particular kind of mental gymnastics. Lately my brain hasn't functioned for the most basic of tasks. In my last months at work I knew I'd have to confess my illness to Ben; my woeful lack of productivity couldn't be hidden anymore. I had tried, very hard, but I could no longer pretend that staring blankly at the computer screen or at pages of reports was the same as actually reading them. My new main 'action' for the day had become making it through to five o'clock.

Ben strode briskly into my office one afternoon, as he often did, a big man with a long list of important things to deal with, someone with eight hundred people to look after, who relied on my support to get things done. 'What are we up to? How's it going?' He rubbed his hands together, preparing for action.

I sat there like a four-day-old balloon, mouth flapping, trying to find the words. 'Um, not that good,' I finally whispered, trying to keep my voice even. *Don't cry. Don't cry.*

He perched on the wall unit opposite, stance softening. 'What's up?'

'I'm just … kind of … um … not coping at the moment.' I kept my eyes fixed on the corner of my desk, trying to numb the emotion as I laid out the reality – how I couldn't think, couldn't function. He listened. 'I've tried all sorts of things but I just … just … ' I shook my head.

'Well, if anyone could have found a solution, you would have,' he said gently. 'Don't worry about this lot.' He stood, briskly scooping up the two piles of reports from my desk. 'I'll take care of it. Just focus on smaller jobs.'

A weight immediately lifted, replaced with overwhelming gratitude for this endlessly reasonable man.

'You should try and get this fixed now, though,' he said, 'before you go on this hike.'

'I'll be all right when I get there.' I was sure of it.

Time passed and I sank further still. I traded photocopying for googling funny animal videos. Sometimes I think Ben saw. In the end we both just pretended I was getting work done.

My brain is definitely functioning better now. But it's still delicate.

~

It takes a day to work through logistics and chores on the streets of Auckland. My hiking pants are so loose I no longer need to undo the zip to pull them down. Canvassers for charity on the street allow me to pass by. Panhandlers ignore me. I mustn't look like I have money to spare.

I hunt down a printer for my next batch of maps but the computer refuses to download the large files and I struggle to control the rising frustration. I head to the supermarket to resupply, weaving my way through heaving footpaths. Someone slows to a halt directly in front of me, engrossed in the screen of a mobile phone. *Get out of the bloody way, dickhead!*

I stop, shocked at the unkind voice in my head, then almost immediately remember it used to be a familiar voice, a voice that commentated my every move before I left home. The realisation that it ever existed, and that it has returned, is alarming.

~

There are 53 kilometres to be walked across greater Auckland in several day hikes, without my pack. They're urban, paved with gravel or concrete, but I want to walk every step of the way, to feel the achievement of knowing I have crossed the entire length of a country under my own steam – one continuous line, in all its beauty and blandness. Cutting corners is not the way I roll.

I start from the hostel but the turn-by-turn instructions are confusing so I switch on my GPS to follow the blue line. It flashes uselessly, claiming not to know where I am. *I'm in Auckland! How can you not know that?* I panic, wondering what's wrong with it, where I can get it fixed, how long it will delay me. I'll be lost without a GPS down south! But then again sometimes I'm lost with it.

I spy khaki in the crowd. What are the odds?

'Liam!'

I catch up to him and hand him the device. Quickly he thumbs through its menus. 'You don't have any cover here. It's probably the buildings.' He gestures at the skyscrapers around us, handing it back to me within seconds.

'Oh. Right. Thanks.' I feel stupid for not knowing.

'We're going out for dinner tonight if you want to join us? Antoine, me and Marcine, another French hiker.'

I take a deep breath, regaining calm. 'Sounds great.'

I wait for them at day's end on a street corner, spying Antoine first, moving through the crowd at his trademark brisk pace. Pen and paper in hand, he stops in front of me. 'Are you Laura Waters?'

'Yes?'

He nods quickly, crossing me off his list of things to do, and I smile. 'In the bush all you have to do is walk,' he laments, massaging his forehead.

I've never seen him look so agitated but I feel the same. The loss of a peaceful environment has corresponded with the loss of a peaceful mind. I've found it hard to cultivate patience and kindness in such a place. A text message from Steve arrives during dinner. *Over all the hustle and bustle of the city yet?* We all feel it.

Antoine, Liam and Marcine plan to leave in the morning, skipping the city to pick up the trail further south, and glumly I realise I am likely doomed to be forever one day behind them. I broach my concerns about walking alone.

'Perhaps we could wait an extra day for you to finish the

city bits …?' Liam speaks quietly, looking around the table at the others, eyebrows raised.

There is no objection. They will wait.

The acrobat grasps the next pair of outstretched arms.

~

The morning is dark. The TV weatherman paints a grim picture, a vast belt of rain sweeping across most of the North Island. But I have 35 kilometres to walk. I stand at the window, taking in the scene below, the traffic lights reflecting distorted streaks of red and green on wet roads. *I could actually do with a rest day.* I'd still be hiking the better part of the country even if I didn't do today's section. Does it really matter if I don't hike every bit? The bed and a bag of chocolate croissants call quietly for my return.

Of course I need to do it!

I bundle up in waterproofs before I can question myself any further, throw essentials into a dry bag and head out into the sheeting rain. My tenacity is rewarded with a tour of South Auckland's sewage oxidation ponds, the airport, a road section through an industrial estate, suburban parkland and finally the botanic gardens. Surprisingly the oxidation ponds prove the highlight of the day, with the surrounding wetlands and waterways flourishing with birds. I see scores of the iconic pukeko, swamp hens flapping low over the water, their red legs dangling awkwardly.

It's a long, wet day but by the end of it I have ticked off every kilometre needed before joining the others. I will stay true to my goal of walking every step.

5

Mud, Moss and Vines

South of Auckland I join Liam, Antoine and Marcine at a picnic table to make dinner and the conversation switches immediately from French to English. I appreciate it but feel self-conscious that it's only for my benefit.

Slowly Liam carves a slice from a lemon with a knife, eating it straight off the blade without flinching.

'Wow! You like lemons, eh?' I'm impressed.

'It's for vitamin C. It's too heavy to be carrying much else fresh.'

'Mm.' I cast an eye over my own pack. 'Actually, I know it's decadent but I need something fresh every day,' I confess, reaching for a bag containing two mandarins, an apple, a small onion and a zucchini.

'Well, I guess you'll have to be more sensible down south.'

South, where the sections are longer, where we'll have to carry more food. I'll see how I go.

Marcine looks over at my camp, pushing her large round glasses up the bridge of her nose. 'Your tent is so small.' It might have been a compliment but for the slight grimace in her smile. I follow her gaze. It *is* small but at least it's light while still being fully sealed against creepy-crawlies. 'All these things …' She waves a hand over my kit, scattered across the table, picking up an almost weightless kitchen cloth and gesturing at a thin face washer and mini chamois towel. If there is a double-up I can't see it. No amount of weight-saving desire could tempt me to wash my cooking pot and utensils with the same cloth I use to clean my acrid armpits and crotch.

Marcine's pack is about half the size of mine. I don't know how she does it. I spent months weighing every single item in my pack and searching the internet for lighter options. I discovered the shortcuts ultralight hikers make but there were few I was prepared to adopt. Sleep in a hammock instead of a tent? It sounded draughty and cold. Cut the handle off my toothbrush? No thanks. Wear a thin down jacket instead of a fat puffy one? I'd never survive. Anyway, I'm happy with what I've got.

I suddenly miss Steve and Brad's laissez-faire attitude.

But I have company. That is the main thing. Mum is happy too. I'm walking with three others and, most importantly, two of them are male. 'I feel better knowing you have Liam and Antoine with you,' she wrote in an email. She doesn't know these men, doesn't know if they are wild risk-takers or foolish idiots, but they *are* men and that's what seems to count.

I know my mum worries about me. I've tested her for years with my solo travel, my scuba diving, snowboarding and occasional skydiving. But I can worry her with much lesser things. Heading out without a jacket. Walking the dog at dusk. A random solitary cough.

They say a problem shared is a problem halved. Unless you share it with my mum, in which case it becomes a problem multiplied by ten as every potential danger and pitfall, no matter how remote, is brought into sharp relief. Her worrying never makes me feel better, only worse. So usually I spare us both the angst and tell her nothing.

It's frustrating but I'm told it's just a mother's love, something I will never understand because I'm forty-three and yet to find a man with whom I want to spend the rest of my life, let alone have a family of my own. I've had boyfriends, lots of them. A good few even talked of marriage but I broke them off, every last one of them. I always thought there was something suspicious about a pattern like that. That surely the law of averages must determine that at some point someone should break up with me instead. I seemed to get myself stuck in relationships, not knowing exactly what love was supposed to feel like but suspecting it wasn't what I had. Then I had to leave them. That took ages. Years, sometimes. Leaving then succumbing again, seesawing in uncertainty, never entirely sure I was making the right decision and hating the thought of the alternative – being alone.

Fifty years my parents were married. Every morning I watched my dad wrap his arms around Mum at the kitchen sink, both of them smiling. 'Love you,' he would say, nuzzling into her ear. Fifty years. That's commitment. That's happiness. *That's love*, I thought.

I never had anything that looked like that.

~

*The track in the southern part of this section
requires good navigation skills. It's marked
but not otherwise formed, and you should be
careful to follow the orange triangles as
there are other tracks that intersect
it en route.*

Marcine screws up her nose at the trail notes for the Hunua Ranges. Forests are too messy for her. She opts for a road detour, joining another French girl, leaving Antoine, Liam and me to climb through them.

Stands of ferns give way to a tangle of thick, cane-like vines, winding up tree trunks into the misty heights and twisting around each other when there is nothing else to cling on to. On the ground they're like a mess of electrical cables, wrapping around my ankles and tripping me up. It all seems ridiculously overdone. We laugh and play around and pretend to garrotte ourselves on the loops that dangle from above. It's funny – for the first hour.

The ground rises and falls in steep undulations, all slippery mud and leaves. The vines ease a little but the ground trail disintegrates. New markers appear – random strips of tape hanging from branches or squares of white metal hammered into trees. *Are they just older markers? Temporary diversions?* We haven't seen an orange triangle in ages. Liam checks his GPS and the pre-programmed TA route seems to align with a rough path ahead marked by strands of pink tape dangling from branches. We hesitate but, with no better alternative, give our trust to the GPS. After twenty minutes the tape, and the path, runs out.

Chaos creeps in. We move in different directions, bush-bashing up and down hills, trying to find something resembling a track. I grunt like a weightlifter from the effort, hauling myself up rocks and roots and vines, yet still our path is elusive. Suddenly I'm not even sure that we will find our way back to the pink tape and a weak panic starts to flutter in my gut at the thought of being properly lost.

Liam stands his ground to study the GPS while I hang my body over my poles to rest. I wipe the sweat from my forehead and suck on the water bladder stowed within my pack but it gurgles back, a mix of water and air. I'm empty. I check the small emergency bottle in the front pocket and discover it is only half full.

'Liam, how much water do you have left?'

'Ah, not much.' He pulls out a plastic bottle with a few mouthfuls in the bottom. Antoine, too, is low.

It's 5.30pm. Even if we *did* know which way to go, there would be at least a good three hours of walking between us and the river at the forest's edge. The seed of panic grows.

'Okay, we can bush-bash down the hill and we'll eventually hit the river and exit the forest,' says Liam. 'We probably won't be on course but at least we'll be out. Or we can go back up the hill to the last orange triangle marker and look harder for the trail.' He's the man who's never flustered, the man who really knows his way around a GPS unit. I feel sure Liam can resolve our predicament, yet neither he nor Antoine seems confident that all will be well. It's unsettling.

I try to weigh up the options and contribute usefully to the debate but the bottom line is I'll do whatever they think. Anyway, my brain has started behaving oddly, hampered by a swirling fog.

Stumbling feet, balance out of whack – with sluggish awareness I realise it's dehydration. Shit.

The decision is made to turn back. I curse the hills and vines and fallen trees with slurred words. Tears of frustration and exhaustion threaten but I fight them back. It would do no good and, anyway, I need every drop of energy focused on escaping the forest.

We find our way back to the last orange marker and there, pointing downhill into the setting sun, is a faint trail that we missed before. We move as fast as we can without running, descending for two toe-jarring hours until the forest opens up to reveal twinkling lights far below. Civilisation!

At nine o'clock we stumble upon an impressive gated driveway, flanked by two warmly glowing coach lights. A sign next to the intercom warns against trespassing and the guys linger behind me – Liam shy, Antoine not confident of his English. I step forward and press the buzzer.

'Hello?' A male voice crackles through the small metal grate.

'Hi. We're three lost hikers, just come out of the Hunua forest. We're out of water and not quite sure where we are.' I notice my voice changing mid-flight, accentuating the tone of a helpless woman in a way that surprises me. *Don't turn us away!*

'Wait a minute,' the voice says.

Footfalls approach from the dark, someone from the 'normal world' who is clean and hydrated and knows where we are. 'I suppose you need somewhere to stay the night too?' The metal gates open with a hum and his face comes into view.

It's a private school camp that was a luxury resort in a previous life. We have a villa, a hot shower. I collapse on its tiles, waving the showerhead weakly over my body, inspecting the wrinkled white soles of my feet, flapping with chunks of skin too deep to pull away. It's agony.

The relief is palpable over dinner. I go over our movements, trying to learn from where we went wrong, how we missed the marker, how we wandered off trail. We should have paid more attention to the trail notes; we were wrong to put all our trust in the GPS. I file the lessons away then wonder what I would have done if I were on my own. What choices would I have made and would they have got me out of the woods before I collapsed with dehydration?

Antoine eyes me seriously for a moment. 'Many girls get upset in this situation, but not you.'

'Yeah, well, I thought about it but I didn't think it would help.'

'Always fresh, always beautiful. Like you just started out for the day.'

I laugh at the lie.

'The only reason I know you are tired is because you start swearing a lot,' he adds.

Now, that's true.

The shared ordeal seems to have bonded us and within half an hour I am wiping tears of laughter from my face – or maybe they're tears of delirium. Whatever. I feel good. I prop my feet up on a dry bag filled with clothes and will the blood to travel away from my aching legs. Tomorrow is another day.

~

After forty days of the trail, we stand with a man and his dog in a hilltop park as he points out the thick green mass of Mount Pirongia in the distance. It's not huge but it's the first obstacle in our way to be called a mountain. There will be more to come, many more. They will get higher, harder, more remote, more exposed. My stomach flutters briefly at the thought but I quiet it with a resolve to tackle things one day at a time. After all, I've already walked 800 kilometres. Who would have thought I'd get this far without Belle? Not me, that's for sure.

I look behind to where we've just walked, then to the mountainous green range ahead. Seeing both aspects at once heightens my awareness of the distance my two legs can cover. I realise that I'm moving forward, travelling south, *getting somewhere*. However slow, it is progress.

~

The track is mostly unformed, with steep,
rough or muddy sections.

I walk on my own for the first day in Pirongia Forest, breaking early from lunch to get going, ahead of the others. I've noticed my mind is quieter when I walk alone, and I like that. There is a peace in being alone, a silence from words spoken and, without the cogs turning for conversation, thought seems to slow down too.

The trail climbs steadily – mud, dirt and tree roots. I pause to feel the texture of bark on a tree and gaze up at the light playing through the canopy above. This solitude is more than a need for peace. I need to know what it's like again to walk solo, to navigate, to be responsible for my own progress. I need to be prepared.

There's a crash in the bushes behind me and I step aside to let Antoine power through at an even faster pace than usual. 'I'm racing Liam to the summit,' he explains breathlessly. Before I can respond, the blue of his t-shirt disappears again into the foliage. Five minutes pass before Liam forges up the trail and in a moment he too is gone.

I wonder if Antoine does anything slowly. I find it tiring sometimes just watching him; everything he does is swift. I admire his ability, though it clashes with my own desire to slow down, to reunite all the pieces of my body and mind, to connect with nature.

A large bird surprises me in the centre of the track. We both pause, the pheasant and I barely a metre apart. One dark shiny eye appraises me, the brown-feathered head tilted, and then the bird returns to fossicking, scuffing around in the leaves, searching for food with a faint noise like a little pheasant twitter of contentment. It feels good to be ignored, to be accepted as a creature of the forest.

But as the hours pass I start to doubt my place here. The trail diminishes to a tangle of tree roots. No trace of Antoine or Liam remains, no reassuring sound of voices filtering through the air. I am alone, buried under the dark canopy. Have I missed a turn-off? No, this has to be it – there is only one trail, and I'm following markers.

Uncertainty lingers.

Go on, Laura. You're the head of this mission. Lead on.

It seems an alien notion. When have I truly led myself? So much of my life has operated like a carriage on tram tracks – in motion yet confined to well-established routes. Like most others in the modern world, I am trained for employment, to be a functioning citizen working under others and trusting they have the bigger picture under control: signs and fences keep me away from danger, and daily decisions are selected from a range of tried and tested options. Being on unfamiliar ground with no clue or backup doesn't happen often.

And when decisions *are* required, it's rare that I'm the one making them. The world I grew up in always had a man at the helm. The office boss, the boyfriend who took control, the father who sat at the head of the table, drove the family car and changed the light bulbs. My mum was very happy with this arrangement. She was happy to be on backup, to be the one handing over cups of coffee and sandwiches while Dad worked on whatever he was doing. She was happy to relinquish all decision making to him, even if on occasion those decisions ultimately turned out to be wrong. If Dad wasn't interested in seeing a particular film she wouldn't see it either.

Leading my own way has never really been on my radar. Until now.

I decide I don't want to be slogging up the wrong hill with energy and daylight steadily draining. I cave in, pausing to switch the GPS on. A little blue triangle shows my position, hovering above a dashed line leading to Mount Pirongia, and relief and disappointment mingle. Why did I doubt myself?

This trail is a piece of cake compared with what lies ahead. I need to lift my game.

The dense forest finally peters out and the mountain hoists me onto its shoulder for an immense view of its green and sprawling bulk. Elation courses through me – at having finally knocked off the long, dark climb and at sharing it with no one but a pheasant.

I watch a dazzling sunset with Liam and Antoine, all of us cooing over its changing light, then retreat to the warmth of my tent. It takes scrolling through photos to see the subtle changes that have taken place within me over the passing weeks. My nightly review of the day's highlights has never yielded more than beautiful landscapes but tonight I notice something different in them, in the photos of *me*. I look back over previous weeks to compare, zooming in to study them better. I look different now somehow. It's not just the smile, which hasn't been seen much in the last year. Is it the tan, maybe? No, it is more than that. My skin looks better. I look lighter.

I finally realise that I look like *me*. Not the 'me' I was familiar with but the *real* me. Someone I had long forgotten existed. A woman unburdened, free from pressures, doing something that makes her happy. When was I last this person? I truly don't remember.

And what of anxiety? With a jolt I recognise I haven't seen it much lately. Nervousness, yes, but not that crippling, all-consuming, chest-squeezing awfulness. Have I escaped that too? Barely six weeks ago I was curled up in a ball on the bed, crying at nothing in particular, hardly able to get through the day without feeling as though my heart would explode or that I might faint from not breathing properly. For a year I have tried herbal drugs, therapy and meditation to relieve the ache, and none of them worked, but put me on a trail in the middle of a forest or beach for a month and I appear to be fine. Surely it couldn't be that straightforward.

And yet here I am. Happy.

I think back, studying my moods over the past weeks. I don't feel that blind anxiety on the trail. I never have. It's other things that make the tightness return – cities, noise, busyness – things I will have to face again at some point.

~

I've already been hiking eleven days straight when we venture into Mahoe Forest. Eleven days of eight to ten hours' walking. Eleven days with trail descriptions such as 'steep, hilly and arduous' on paths so overgrown that I didn't so much see them as sense them.

I enter Mahoe Forest already deeply drained, on a track so overrun there's barely room for me get through. Tiny spikes on thread-like vines latch on to me. The scratch of gorse sends blood trickling down my forearm. A tree branch catches in my hair, breaking off a hefty chunk, which dangles ridiculously from my braids. If it didn't piss me off so much it would be funny. *I just want a path that is wide enough for my feet and has space for my head to pass through! Is that too much to ask?*

Liam and Antoine move fast, still fresh from their extended break in Auckland, their long legs skimming effortlessly over obstacles. I struggle to keep them in sight. If I lose them I might also lose the trail. The track becomes narrower still, off camber, just wide enough for one boot and made worse by fallen trees.

Gotta keep the guys in sight.

I push on as quickly as I can – over a log, through bushes, over another log. A tree branch whips back, slapping me in the face for the umpteenth time just as I slip, falling heavily onto a tangle of rocks and roots. I drag myself to my feet, breathing heavily.

Come on, Laura, stay focused.

I urge my body to keep going but it's no use – the emotion demands a hearing. I stop walking, lift my face to the treetops and let the tears fall.

Have I ever felt so utterly stuffed, so utterly beaten into submission?

I try to swallow the sobs and wipe the tears away – *I have to keep moving!* – but more come. I run a finger over the dried blood on my forearm. My poor body. I've pushed it through so much, fed it nowhere near enough calories for the daily output it gives me. It needs rest.

Liam and Antoine are long gone. I stand still for minutes, dabbing uselessly at my eyes with a tissue, trying to stem the flow, anxious that one of them might come back to look for me. I don't want them to see me like this – weak, crying, broken – but even as this thought passes through my mind another one follows right behind. *No one's coming back for you, Laura.*

The eleven-hour ordeal ends in tiny Waitomo, famed for its underground glow-worm caves, and I call for a day of rest.

Mercifully Liam and Antoine agree to it. A week and a half's accumulated dirt, blood and sweat wash off in the shower, and a rancid stench rises on the steam. I feast on lamb, vegetables, salad and wine. I relax in the warmth of the sun and then delve underground to marvel at the twinkling silvery green sparkles of thousands of glow-worms. I eat as much nourishing food as I can and slowly, slowly, my joie de vivre returns.

~

Liam and I are walking side by side on a gravel back-country road when he drops the bombshell.

'I'd like to walk on my own at some point,' he says casually.

'Oh, right.' I try to match his nonchalance.

'Yeah, I mean, I like walking in a group but at some point I'd like to do a stretch on my own too.'

'Yeah.' *When? Where?*

I can't blame him. He'd arrived in this country alone but somehow, before he even set foot on the trail, his solitude was hijacked. No doubt it would be good for me to hike on my own too – for the challenge, the solitude, for a different experience – but there is no way I'm going to volunteer myself for it.

I wonder where he will bail. Liam wants company down south as much as the rest of us. In the south the land is more rugged, exposed and riddled with unbridged rivers. There'll be far longer stretches between civilisation and no help around for miles. Rarely does anyone explicitly mention it but I sense amongst hikers a wary respect for what is to come.

'Ah, I don't really like these road sections,' he mutters under his breath.

'Oh, they're all right. You just need to listen to some music, then they're fun,' I say, trying to sell him on the idea.

'I'm only doing them because you guys want to walk them.'

I know he is. A few times he's suggested hitching but I've resisted, wanting to stay true to my goal of walking every step. There aren't many roads to walk but the trail is young and the route requires a few of them until further wilderness links are developed. Mostly they are rarely used back roads, through picturesque countryside, but a few are more major. I have considered rethinking my policy, wondered whether it would matter over the course of 3000 kilometres if I missed the odd fifteen or thirty here and there. There's been pressure. For the moment, though, we walk together, every step.

The conversation graduates from logistics to more personal things – home, family, ambitions. Amidst the bare landscape he seems extra tall, extra broad-shouldered, and suddenly I feel shy next to him, as though on a first date. Somehow it's our first proper conversation even though we've walked together for two weeks.

He says he's thinking of writing a book about the hike, an idea that both surprises and interests me. A book would give me an insight into his thoughts, something I haven't yet achieved in real life.

Liam is shy too. Currently single. I wonder if his romantic history is anything like mine – a late bloomer, sweet sixteen and never been kissed. *Surely* this *is the year!* I thought to myself at age twelve. If I knew then that I would have to wait until sixteen for my first kiss I'd have been miserable. If I knew at sixteen that I'd still be unmarried at forty-three I'd probably have topped myself. My sister married at twenty-two, my brother at twenty-four. Things were different back then. In my youth I saw billboards outside pubs advertising party nights for 'over 30s'. *What kind of loser is still single at thirty?* I scoffed to myself. Me, as it turned out.

The available fish in the sea diminish with the passing years, something that no doubt contributed to my persistence with Frank. It seemed easier to try to make things work rather than search anew. We were a good fit on paper: we shared dreams and interests; I loved him (I thought), he loved me (he said). There were moments, albeit brief, when I was grateful for our partnership. Like when he pampered me with a delicious homemade dinner or washed my car, or got rid of a spider that had found its way indoors while I shrieked in a corner. One day when I was down he suggested we take off on a holiday, go somewhere sunny and warm, for some quality time together. It never happened but for that afternoon at least I could live in optimism that all was well.

I didn't want to give it all away when it seemed there was just *one thing* at the root of all our problems. He shared nothing with me but I started to suspect he was just as scared as I was to be vulnerable, just as scared of being judged or rejected – maybe more so. I lay in bed one night, staring blankly, glazed with weariness. I watched him walk from the bathroom to the bedroom, towel wrapped around his waist. 'What are you looking at?' he said suddenly, a hint of panic in his face. He glanced down at his chest, his arms, shifting awkwardly on his feet as though readying himself for something. When his eyes returned to mine they looked desperate.

'Uh, nothing?'

Days later I found him doing bicep curls on the back porch, hauling weights far too heavy for him, his whole body rocking and swaying in a rhythmic ripple. 'Why don't you try smaller weights and then you can focus on isolating the right muscles?' I offered. I don't remember what he grunted in reply but from then on he only worked out when I wasn't looking, doing push ups behind the kitchen counter and jumping to attention when I walked in, pretending there was nothing of interest occurring on the tiles beyond. 'Well, you don't want me to exercise!' he huffed.

It made no sense. I wondered where these random ideas came from. *Stop judging yourself*, I wanted to say. *And stop judging me.*

The gravel road stretches on for hours, skirting huge farms. Quad bikes zip past, ducking from one driveway to the next, with a dog or two sitting up back or maybe a sheep stuffed in the footwell, jammed between the knees of a farmer. Te Kuiti is close now, a tiny town with a big title – sheep-shearing capital of the world. There are five sheep to every person in New Zealand and lately the air has sounded with the whistles of herders and the barks of their dogs, chasing white flocks up and down the hills.

The sun sinks along with our water supplies but there isn't a river for another 20 kilometres, or space to set up a tent. The quest for a solution leads us up a long, winding driveway to a farm, and there we stay. Mary-Anne ushers us one at a time into the shower while Allan pulls out maps and photos of their massive property, and together they explain the intricacies of sheep farming. At dawn fifteen trucks and a light plane arrive to dump fertiliser over the vast acreage, which holds nearly two thousand sheep, in an exhilarating display of aerial skill. Mary-Anne takes us on a tour, bouncing over rough tracks in an open jeep while the plane buzzes just metres above our heads. We pass sheep corralled in holding yards, and the dogs that herded them, their snouts poking out from pens.

When the sun rises higher and the day begins in earnest, Allan sees us off with a handful of fresh strawberries plucked straight from the garden, dropping them into our open palms as we crunch back down the gravel driveway.

'You see, Liam? If we skipped road we'd miss out on meeting people like that!'

'Ah, it was good, all right,' he says quietly, not wanting to concede too much.

'I mean, how awesome! An inside tour on a proper Kiwi sheep farm!'

Days later we meet more locals, a gang of Māori sheep shearers cracking beers the night before a job. They dish out cold cans and hot showers and we learn another piece of the sheep-farming picture. With tents pitched amongst tufts of wool beside the shearing sheds, we fall asleep to the sound of distant bleating.

As I drift off, I feel grateful for these encounters. They connect us, bridge cultures and warm our hearts from the moments we share. Missing the roads would be to rush to the end, to presume that we know what is worth doing and what is not before we've even experienced it.

I want to walk it all.

~

Five days before Christmas we are very nearly a third of the way. I find it hard to comprehend, as though my spindly legs couldn't have actually carried me such a distance, or maybe I've made a mistake in the calculations somewhere. But, no, we've done it.

My body seems to be faltering, though, a more persistent kind of weariness setting in. I keep walking with Antoine and Liam, much to my mother's relief. Nearly every email I receive from her enquires as to their whereabouts. I roll my eyes as I type the words out yet again: '*Yes, Mum, we are still together.*'

'*Oh, good,*' she responds, '*I feel better knowing they are with you.*'

I feel good with them too. We are a team. I feel secure, part of something. Every night Antoine asks Liam and me, 'What time are we leaving tomorrow?' so that he knows what time to get up. We discuss how far we will go, where we will camp.

The kilometres clock over – 900, 1000.

In the middle of beautiful native forest we suddenly stumble across a vast clearing, the land scarred and barren, fringed by stacks of giant trees stripped of their bark and branches, heads lopped off. It's like a scene of mass killing. Pale trunks lie like bodies, piled high, and behind them a long blue truck with a mighty silver grille waits to carry away the fallen. I feel slightly sick.

My beautiful friends, which have sheltered me, dead at the hands of a chainsaw. I feel conflicted, knowing I am part of this story, a consumer, though a deeper part of me feels the mass carnage is somehow intrinsically wrong. I am reminded of the interconnectedness of all living things.

People haven't been in New Zealand for very long in the grand scheme of things. A thousand years ago, with Europe in full swing, New Zealand was still empty of human life. Untouched, it developed into something unique and glorious. Forests flourished with weird and wonderful creatures – frogs, insects, the prehistoric tuatara, and birds, so many birds. Many of them were flightless – the kiwi, takahe, penguins and the clumsy kakapo parrot. There were no mammals at all except for bats, in the air, and whales, dolphins, seals and sea lions, in the sea. I'd love to have seen the place in those times.

Then people arrived. The Polynesians came first, sailing ashore around 1200–1300, and the population of moa – a chunky, long-necked bird, some twice the height of humans – was hunted to extinction. Five hundred years later Europeans started introducing pigs, mice, rats, stoats, possums and rabbits. The invaders swarmed the forests, breeding and hunting, quickly decimating ground-dwelling birds and their eggs. Europeans also introduced deer, which fast bred out of control, damaging the forests relied upon by every other animal; it was barely a few decades later that they were trying to get rid of them again. Teams of deer cullers were set up across the country with trails and huts built to support their movement across the land. Many of those trails and huts are the same ones that hikers use now. Humans haven't been here long but we've made our mark.

Beyond the logging site we return to forest, one of the most beautiful yet. The Pureora welcomes us warmly. There's no gorse, no vines, no hidden holes, just a padded leafy floor winding its way past trees so gnarled and full of character I half-expect them to come to life and start speaking. Wrinkled arms poke out of fat bodies and the deep creases in their trunks could easily be smiling mouths and eyes. Great flaps of moss hang from branches, like the fur on an orangutan's arm. I stop often to take it all in. Even Antoine and Liam slow down.

From Mount Pureora's summit I spy the distant blue of Lake Taupo, the country's largest lake, nestled in the caldera of Taupo Volcano and, to the south, the sprawling, snow-capped peak of Mount Ruapehu, one of the world's most active volcanoes. The scenery is changing, the beaches and dense forests of Northland giving way to alpine landscapes. We are being drawn in, closer to the mountains that will test us.

Bog Inn is home for the night, one of nearly a thousand back-country huts scattered across New Zealand. It's a simple structure of corrugated iron with wooden floorboards, four bunk beds and a fireplace that glows with the warmth of a flickering flame. In its visitor intentions book is an entry from Steve and Brad, dated today.

Damn! We've just missed them. They must have dropped in at lunchtime and kept moving. I can't keep track of them. They skip road, stop to meet friends – they're on a mission of their own design. We could be so close and yet still so far away unless our paths actually cross.

~

In the middle of the Pureora, Liam drops his pack. 'I'm going to have a swim.' He pulls off his boots and wades into a river fully clothed, allowing his body to sink under the surface.

Antoine is ahead but the clear water is too good to pass up. I strip down to underwear and a t-shirt and hobble gingerly over the rounded river stones to the water's edge.

'Ah, you can take your clothes off, if you like. I'm blind without my glasses.' He waves a hand dismissively, turning away.

I study him out of the corner of my eye, not entirely convinced, then shuffle my toes into the water. The cold takes my breath away. Liam's already reclined in a shallow pool, fully immersed save for his head and feet bobbing at the surface. Not one peep of surprise escaped him at the chilly temperature, not even the tiniest gasp. I don't know how he does it. He reminds me of a James Bond villain – bitter lemons, freezing water, nothing seems to shatter his composure.

I study him with a mix of wonder and envy and then suddenly feel self-conscious, alone with him and in my knickers. He is a relative stranger. Who is the man behind the khaki, behind the poker face? Who *is* this guy?

6

Walking on Water

I get to the post office in Taumarunui just before closing on Christmas Eve. The girls in the office back home have posted me the latest set of maps and trail notes but the parcel I collect is far too big for the sheaf of papers I am expecting. It can mean only one thing. Haigh's.

My favourite chocolate shop is next door to the office in Melbourne. I used to visit it a few afternoons a week, slinking out to pick up a bag of gear, something to get me through the day, to make office life more bearable. We were all on it. Orders were put in with whoever was doing a run, scores shared surreptitiously under desks.

I rip into the satchel, pushing past the maps to see the familiar gold logo shining back at me. *Yesss*. They are four bags of my favourites – Berrychocs, a bag each of milk and peppermint pastilles, and another of freckles that have moulded together into one solid slab from the recent Melbourne heat wave. It's a full kilo. It'd be wise to make a decent dent in it tonight.

Also tucked inside is a Christmas card filled with scribbled messages of praise and encouragement. I scan over them, laughing out loud at some and warmed by others. It feels strange reading words that seem to have come from another planet, a world of carpet and plastic, humming with photocopiers and phones. I think of my empty desk, waiting patiently for my return, for me to finish traipsing around the countryside so I can go and do again what I did before. It turns my stomach.

I *used* to like it. But, bit by bit, the role that had once seemed kind of cool started to feel a little empty. Meetings bothered me, uncomfortable corporate clothing bothered me, corporate jargon bothered me. I was tired of hearing about *leveraging, strategic fits, stakeholders* and *low-hanging fruit*.

Office management falls under my role and, with that, policies and procedures. I am yet to come across a more soul-destroying pastime than developing and writing office policies and procedures that no one will ever read. But it is my job so I do it. And everyone still comes to ask me how to do things. And everyone still does things their own way. I think my colleagues believe I am truly passionate about electronic filing folder structures and records maintenance, but in truth I am passionate about ensuring my job, ergo my life, has meaning.

Next to this wild and green life I have been leading, that old world seems even more farcical. The corporate path, which I once forged with such drive and surety, seems to be fading like a track in the forest, withering to nothing and leaving me unsure about where to go next. Wondering where I was even headed in the first place.

~

Steve calls to wish me a happy Christmas, voice puffing down the phone as he walks. 'Brad says, "What up."' They're behind us again after a night with Steve's brother. It's nice of him to call, nice to hear his voice.

I have a lengthy conversation with Belle. The frustration I'd felt at her pulling out has diminished with time and it feels good to exchange stories. She's been having a tough time – a string of illnesses, some very serious, eleven days in hospital. I feel bad for having doubted her.

I phone Mum to wish her a merry Christmas, interrupting the rolling of pastry for a lemon meringue pie. I'll be missing out on the family lunch. A kitchen filled with laughter, dogs racing around the living room tearing up wrapping paper, hot weather, cold champagne and enough food to feed an army. Instead, Christmas Day is a 32-kilometre hike in drizzling rain onto the 42 Traverse – an old logging road named after the original 'State Forest 42' – followed by dehydrated pasta carbonara with a capsicum chopped into it. Distanced from Liam and Antoine by a moat of rainwater, I lie holed up in my tent, dropping Berrychocs into my mouth and re-reading my Christmas card. It's austere but I am content.

The next day it's still drizzling and as I walk I discover I'm angry. Maybe it's because of Christmas – the thought of family and love and what love should be. I stamp my feet on the luscious dark soil and bash the green ferns aside with my poles as little moments keep replaying in my head. Like the time I bought Frank a plane ticket to Queensland for my niece's wedding and he sighed and rolled his eyes the whole time, as though eating and drinking under the palm trees were a great burden to him, a favour I would need to repay.

Or the time I withdrew $20,000 from a savings account to help him meet a loan deadline and it took him nine months to even begin paying it back. I saw the new iMac in the spare room, sleek and shiny with a huge 27-inch screen. I remember feeling awkward asking when he might be able to repay me. 'You asking me about this money is driving a wedge between us!' he yelled in reply, a ridiculous call in light of the chasm that already existed.

Then, months later, the dinner party, Frank the Successful, boasting of his latest acquisition, of his acumen. 'I'm paying double back on my home loan to get ahead,' he said to our table of friends. I looked up from my plate in shock at the stranger opposite, unable to fathom his words. When everyone had gone I confronted him. He'd paid money to the bank on a twenty-year loan before repaying his girlfriend, his girlfriend who was *losing* interest on her own savings to help him? 'Oh, it's probably not the best,' he laughed lightly, smoothing things over as he always did, trying to make the not-okay okay.

The most annoying thing was being the only witness to the truth of him. I wished that at home he was the person he became when there was an audience. With people around he would smile tenderly at me, speak lovingly, rub my arm softly. I could find no pattern in his words and ways, no stability that made clear where I stood. It enraged me. I was a hooked fish, reeled in, run out, reeled in again, until every last drop of fight was taken from me.

He once said he'd thought about proposing to me on New Year's Eve. I'm not sure why he told me that. Perhaps he hoped to get brownie points for simply considering it. Thank God he didn't.

Mother*fucker*.

I pause to breathe, trying to redirect my focus to the trail, trying to be present. *Let go of the anger, Laura, it doesn't serve you.*

~

A river looms. A big one. In less than a week we must paddle it for a few hundred kilometres, an official part of the trail. The Whanganui is New Zealand's third-longest, gathering water from the peaks of Ruapehu, Tongariro and Ngauruhoe before flowing through the Central Volcanic Plateau in the middle of the North Island south to the sea.

We wander amidst these volcanoes to traverse the high alpine desert of the Tongariro Crossing. This is *Lord of the Rings* territory, a vast and surreal moonscape dotted with blue and green lakes and the cone of Mount Ngauruhoe – Mount Doom. Outcrops of rock, tinged red with iron, push through dark grey sand under a blanket of icy fog. It's mystical. Scale and distance is hard to grasp in the desert's vast spaces. From high ridges of rocky scoria, the figures of day hikers in the valleys below appear like a line of ants. Even without bright sunlight the three crater pools of the Emerald Lakes seem to glow, fringed in sulphurous yellow and generating their own light and colour. Tinted by minerals leached from the surrounding thermal areas, they appear like sunken pockets of brightly coloured enamel in an otherwise metallic grey landscape. It's barren but beautiful.

~

Potential hazards: don't canoe the river
when water levels are rising or it's in flood.
If you capsize you may not be able to get
back in or swim to the river's edge.

Taumarunui is our entry point. The night before departure I crouch in a shipping container on the water's edge, cooking noodles and listening to the thundering rain on the steel roof. What will the extra deluge of water do to the river? Raise the rapids by a grade or two? Throw in a few extra logs, perhaps?

The rain is so loud we can hardly hear each other speak.

'Okay, so you're after two canoes and one kayak, yeah?' Ron yells over the din, his alert eyes darting between us.

'Ah, I don't think we're completely decided yet.' I turn to the group. 'Who wanted to be sharing a canoe?'

'I don't know.' Liam looks around.

'I don't mind kayaking. I've done a bit of it before.' Summer's voice is so soft it barely registers above the rainwater rushing over the open edge of the shelter. I haven't seen her for six weeks. Her Te Araroa dream is over but she's joined us to paddle and I'm glad for her company.

'What's more stable?' I ask Ron.

'The kayaks will go faster than the canoes and they're a bit easier to manoeuvre, but you can get more gear in the canoes, stretch out a bit. If you take a sit-in kayak, your body will stay drier with the neoprene spray deck. With the sit-*on* kayaks, there's no spray deck but it's easier to get back on board if you flip over,' he says.

May that never happen, I silently wish.

'We only rent out sit-in kayaks if you've flipped a kayak before and know how to release the spray deck from the cockpit.'

That's me. My limited whitewater experience includes a backward flip on a river thirteen years ago. I came around a bend, the swift current sweeping me towards a huge log stretched horizontally just above the surface. I dumped my paddle and blocked my face in preparation for impact, and the moment summoned razor-sharp focus. *This could be it*, I thought. Rivers are often clogged with submerged trees and branches, a potentially lethal trap for anyone who might collide with them, but to my deep gratitude the water under the log was clear and I resurfaced, flooded with adrenaline but alive.

In the grand scheme of things the rapids we will face are relatively tame, but we are without a guide and are no experts. They will still test us. No operator will rent a boat to a solo traveller so Mason, our reluctant teammate from the northern forests, has returned to the fold, bringing our party to five.

'I'm taking a kayak, you guys can do what you want,' he says abruptly, walking outside, escaping to the container next door.

'Ah, I don't know what the problem is,' Liam says quietly once he's gone.

There were a lot of factors to consider in the planning of our river passage. It wasn't exactly difficult to reach agreement on these things but it wasn't a quick process and the required collaboration seemed to test Mason.

Liam, Antoine, Mason and I sat on the floor of our room in Taumarunui a week ago, nutting out the details, surrounded by maps and boat rental leaflets. Perhaps if we'd just gone along with the plan Mason had spent days researching everything would have been okay but we each wanted to understand it, to decide whether we were happy to put in above the most difficult set of rapids or to enter further down the river instead, each wondering how far we would be able to paddle in a day, what date we should ask to be collected at the finish.

'I've already asked Luke and Kendall. They went through a few weeks ago and said the upper rapids were fine,' Mason said.

'Ah, but Marcine and Joelle were told by another operator it was too dangerous for them,' said Antoine.

We discussed the options, expressed our concerns and thoughts. We each needed to weigh it up. Perhaps we should go and talk directly with the boat operator, we wondered.

'You see,' Mason sputtered, 'this is the problem!'

Quietly we continued our discussion.

'Antoine, what do you think? Are you comfortable going in here? Have you paddled before?' I asked.

'No. I never paddle before.' He frowned, unsure.

'Everyone's getting stressed!' Mason's voice rose above ours.

'No one's getting stressed!' *Except you.* I bit back the words that would only have made things worse. But I'd raised my voice, fed up with how his company reminded me of Frank's. How it took me back to living with a stress-head, a storm in his own teacup. I was still raw, my tolerance stretched. I snapped and it broke things, the veneer of pleasantries shattered. Now, more than ever, it was clear Mason would rather be alone. But he cannot hire a boat without us.

The rain thunders down.

'After this section we'll probably spread out a bit, yes?' Liam's expression gives nothing away.

Is he talking about Mason or does he want to split from me and Antoine too? I don't know what to say so I just squat on the damp floor, stirring my noodles, watching the rain.

Antoine drags a kayak into a newly formed lake on the grass, climbing aboard to do a few mock strokes of the paddle. In the end we decide there will be no canoes. We will all fly solo, taking our chances, piloting our own way down the river.

The rain continues all evening. I lie in my tent listening to water pinging off the flysheet and the rush of the river below. My stomach is tight. Tomorrow we plunge into the unknown. Once we push off we'll be funnelled into a series of gorges largely inaccessible by land; tomorrow alone there will be well over fifty rapids to face.

Memories of my last whitewater outing resurface. It's the unknown that unsettles me. Everything is fine – until something goes wrong. I pull out my Christmas card again and re-read the messages. They give me a boost, like a little cheerleading team on the banks of the river.

Why do I always doubt myself? There is no reason I can't do this like everyone expects me to. I try to rewrite my old beliefs, silently running my positive-thinking mantra through my head. *I'm a fucking legend, I'm a fucking legend.*

I want to know what will happen, how it will all pan out. But life doesn't work that way. I will just need to take a leap of faith and hope that a net will catch me.

The rain sheets down and a faint memory arises – the time our family camped in the shadow of the Hume Dam, our tent pitched beneath a mighty concrete wall that held back a body of water six times the volume of Sydney Harbour. It bucketed down with rain all night while my mother kept vigil, convinced the wall would burst. She ran an escape plan through her mind, right down to which parent would grab which child. The dog would have to fend for herself. If Mum were here now she would surely worry the river would burst its banks.

All around me is quiet except for the sound of water. What are the others thinking in their tents? Are they apprehensive too or are they sleeping soundly? I'm alone in my world of unease, a world in my head, a world only I have control over.

I reassure myself with the fact that we have the blessing of the expert on this river, the nice man lending us his boats. Surely Ron wouldn't let us go if he didn't think we could do it safely.

I lie there in the dark, waiting. Slowly, gradually, the fog in my brain begins to clear. I just need to trust.

~

The river flows dark and fast in the morning, higher against the bank than it was yesterday. Only a few sporadic raindrops remain. Ron briefs us in a sprawling house overlooking the river, black marker squeaking over a whiteboard as he quickly sketches out scenarios and how we should tackle them. Squiggles indicate boulders and river bends; the water flow is indicated by different sized Vs. We should always aim for the biggest V, where the water flows at its widest and most powerful. If our boats collide against a boulder we should lean away from it, allowing the water to lift us off our perch and push us onwards. These nuggets of wisdom, critical to our safety, are fired out in quick succession. I dare not forget any of them.

We huddle to watch video footage of the river on a computer, mostly on fast-forward but slowed at points of interest. Major hazards, exits for campsites – we need to know what they look like from water level. Six days of river breezes by in twenty minutes and the influx of information seems far too copious to remember but Ron assures us it is all now subliminally embedded in our heads, ready to surface again at the required moment.

Kitted out in helmet and life jacket, I settle myself in the cockpit of my kayak. I give the riverbank a few nudges with my paddle and shuffle in the seat until the water lifts me into the current, its powerful flow drawing us quietly into the heart of the Whanganui.

Immediately it's peaceful. I stare in wonder at my new path, its dark flow cutting a corridor through dense greenery. The paddle slices the water cleanly, moisture dripping off the ends and sending tiny beads bouncing along the surface like mercury. Pale, creamy brown blobs float on the surface and I assume they are foam until they bounce against each other with a clink and scrape. Volcanic pumice! I push them underwater with my fingers and then watch them bob back up. I drop them from the height of an outstretched arm but still they float. Scooping up a handful of the pebbles, I throw them at Antoine and Summer just as they discover them, and a pumice fight ensues.

A faint rushing floats on the breeze, growing louder by the moment. Rapids. We round a bed and the gurgling water comes into view, the rush now a roar. I sit as tall as I can, nervously straining for a visual on the flow.

'Left or right?' Antoine shouts.

What would I know?

The water sucks us in, closer, faster.

Mason takes the lead, choosing a line and dipping down into the rapid, his boat suddenly accelerated by the flow. He emerges on the other side unscathed so I follow his line, bouncing along the path of least resistance. 'Woo hoo!'

Hoots of exhilaration echo behind me as the others follow.

More rapids appear, one after the other, and a tiny bud of confidence blooms as the fear ebbs – the unknown becoming known.

The river quickens, descending out of sight, just a line of white foam. It's not easy to see how big the rapids are or where the all-important 'V' is. There is no option but to choose a line and commit to it, making adjustments as needed. Waves smash from each side and I press on the water with my paddle for balance. Dab, dab, dab – two quick strokes to the left, one to the right. *Come on, come on, focus!*

The bow pierces a series of chocolate-coloured waves, seemingly static in the current, sending a wash of water over the deck and slamming into my chest. The river is both exhilarating and heart-stopping. I barely have time to bask in the success of small achievements before the next challenge appears but with every rapid my confidence grows.

I think of my brother and dad who raced kayaks through gates on whitewater rivers years ago. I can see why they liked it so much. The Boy Scouts had introduced them to it and, with high hopes of doing something similarly exciting, I had joined the Girl Guides, but instead of paddling I was given instruction on how to cook a doughy pancake on an upturned tin can with a candle underneath, or how best to trim and shape my fingernails. It was a massive disappointment.

The flow eases for a spell, carrying us gently through steep-sided gorges carpeted in moss. At last I can study the river's beauty. I lean back in my seat for a better view of the draping tree ferns, the kingfishers gliding and diving, the waterfalls bursting through foliage to rain into the river. Some are hidden, their presence only given away by a thunderous roar escaping from a crack in the rock.

There's immense beauty all around but as I paddle I notice that the air isn't quite making its way to the bottom of my lungs. Every swallow I take has to force a way through my ever-tightening throat. I groan, weary of the recurrence. I'm in paradise, feeling an exhilaration I haven't felt in ages, and still anxiety pays me a visit. It can't be about the river. I don't feel scared anymore. What is it?

Despite my best efforts to remove him from my mind, I felt Frank needling his way back in as the river drew closer, his memory growing larger still when it finally appeared. The last time I sat in a kayak was with him – an overnight trip on an enormous alpine lake in New Zealand. We'd arrived under ominous graphite clouds and a fierce wind. 'We've got to get across this water and set up camp before the waves get bigger.' Frank's face was lined with worry. 'The water's only about five degrees here. If we fall out in the middle we could die,' he said dramatically, eyes darting over the expanse of whitecaps.

I grabbed one end of his fully laden kayak and helped him carry it to the water's edge before heading back to retrieve my own. When I reached it he was no longer with me. I turned to see him paddling frantically away from shore. I couldn't fathom how I could be in a relationship, live with someone for years, and yet feel so alone.

The metal shell of an old car suddenly appears in the middle of the river, almost obscured by foliage and collected flotsam, and something inside urges me to pay attention. Ah yes, the car! It means that our campsite is just around the corner. Ron's subliminal programming seems to be working.

~

I wake up sobbing into my inflatable pillow. A dream. Something to do with Frank. Some pain, long stored, is trying to work its way out. I crawl outside my tent and take comfort from the sun's early morning warmth, then notice Mason's tent has gone. He's left without us.

It takes five hours to cover the next 32 kilometres to Mangapapa camp. There are fewer big rapids, though the walls of rock close in tighter around us, squeezing the river. I whizz past solid rock feeling flimsy and vulnerable. Giant boulders hidden far beneath the surface disrupt the water, sending us spinning from left to right like cars on a skidpan. The river's power smashes any illusions of control I might like to imagine I have in navigating it. At the end of the day I am carried at its whim.

When the water relaxes again I paddle side by side with Summer, each of us debriefing on our recent failed relationships. It's cathartic to finally talk about it, helping to defuse old emotions, but I feel bad for unloading on her.

I never wanted to tell anybody much about our relationship when I was actually in it – not friends or family. I don't really like to get advice from others. They don't know the whole story; they see things through the prism of their own experiences and values. If I revealed the full extent of our challenges they'd question why I was with him, without seeing that he had issues of his own, that he was trying, that we all are. Besides, if I left him it would mean starting all over again, going back to the drawing board. It would mean that everything I had invested – suffered – to that point had been for nothing. It seemed something I had to work out for myself, without others' opinions, without help.

But perhaps I should have talked to them. Then they would have said what they told me after I left. That they'd never liked him. That they thought he was intense, shallow, weird. It might have been enough to nudge me over the line, to save myself in time.

The only person I really shared everything with was Adam. I sat down in his plush chair as he enquired, in a soft and soothing voice, as to what had brought me there. It felt so clichéd I laughed out loud.

'I've never done this before,' I said.

'Is that so?' He smiled at me curiously. The question lingered in the air and I realised that everything I said would be weighed for potential deeper meaning.

Conscious of the hefty price tag on my one-hour session, I fired out my story in the most succinct way I could while Adam's eyes progressively widened in a way that seemed to confirm things had indeed been as bad as I'd felt. He shifted in his chair at the end of it.

'Well, firstly, your body …' He waved a hand up and down my frame, searching for appropriate words. 'There's obviously no problem there.' We both smiled, awkward.

He continued, trying to loosen the pain that had lodged itself within. 'I think we need to look at why you chose to stay with him,' he said kindly, his words hinting at the work that needed to be done. Self-belief. Self-worth.

He was too late to guide me though my relationship – by then I'd already left Frank. What I desperately needed was a way to relax, to purge the pain. But that was turning out to be a much bigger job.

~

We glide between sheer rock walls. No one dips a paddle. The silence and overwhelming beauty has calmed us. We float, paddles rested across laps, gazing upwards, but my body is still tense, my chest tight, each swallow uncomfortable. I put in a few quiet paddle strokes to distance myself from the others. Whatever emotion I am holding on to needs to come out. If I can't heal myself out here I won't be able to do it back home. It's too busy there, noisy. There are pressures to deal with. At home there will be no time. *Release it*, I beg my body, the universe, anyone who is listening. I slump in the cockpit and a few sobbing tears fall down my cheeks.

I keep paddling slowly, aware of the river through blurred eyes, the water, the trees, birdsong.

Shhhhh, the wind says.

It seems ancient and perennial. Calm. There is nothing unnecessary here. Nature has no baggage; it exists in the now, while I am a bundle of noise created from the pain of the past. Perhaps if I can tune myself to nature's frequency then I, too, might be calm. I could transform the scattered, fragmented energy within me to a solid and coherent one. Clear. Thinking and doing only what is necessary, without complication.

I consciously try to shift my thoughts from Frank to the river and in doing so notice that I can actually *feel* the stillness of the rock, the soft flow of water, the music of the birds. The swiftness of the mental shift is a surprise.

~

On New Year's Eve we drag our boats up a bank and climb to a small terrace overlooking the river. I flop onto the grass in the sun, flicking through the set of laminated maps and notes that Ron gave us, outlining every one of the 239 named and numbered rapids we will encounter. It's a nice idea though I can't imagine ever reading them while racing through them. 'When river is low go left of big rock 2nd rapid past Ngaporo,' says one. 'At low flows a shallow shingle bar R causes a deceiving current that quickly moves craft towards a snag L. Keep as far R as possible.' I scan through them, hoping to subliminally absorb some of it.

A chatty Kiwi couple set up a tent next to mine. 'Oh, we met a few other hikers this afternoon!' says the girl. 'They're doing the same trail as you, I think. They're at Whakahoro, just a little way back.' She waves an arm upstream.

'Oh, really? Do you know who they were?'

'Two guys. One Kiwi and the other from the States, I think. They were staying at Whakahoro.'

Steve and Brad. My heart jumps, swiftly followed by disappointment. They could barely be five kilometres away. It's a shame not to be celebrating the new year with them. Surely on an evening like this I could have got a kiss from Steve. That's what New Years are all about – hiding under the cover of darkness and alcohol, all responsibility for the future relinquished – a kiss without consequences. Oh well.

I fish a bottle of red wine from my boat and join Liam, Antoine and Summer at a picnic table covered in drinks and chips and chocolate-coated peanuts. Mason hovers on the fringe, steadily munching his way through a packet of biscuits and looking slightly grumpy, wary about joining in, as though there might be some catch. I wonder what's going on in his head, why he distances himself.

A new girl drifts over to join us – quiet, smiling, her short brown curls tied back in a tiny ponytail. Isabel is my age and from Berlin. A solo traveller, she has been paired up by the rental company to share a canoe with an older American she didn't know until a few days ago. Bob is a kind man but he can really talk. I know because I've already spent twenty minutes cornered by him at the supermarket in Taumarunui, waiting for a pause in the monologue to excuse myself. And now Isabel is sharing a space of about four metres squared with him for days on end.

'How's it going?' I ask.

'Yeah, it's going okay.' She nods slowly, a little smile playing on her lips. 'So are you walking on your own?'

'Sort of. I started out with a friend but she pulled out on the second day.'

'I heard about you! I stayed with Mary in Ngunguru. She talked a lot about you.'

I pause while the penny drops. 'Oh, you stayed there too!' Mary emailed me weeks ago after finding two more girls with backpacks wandering the streets. 'So are you the writer or the scientist?' I ask keenly. Either would be interesting.

'The writer.' She smiles.

'Cool,' I say. 'I'd like to write too.'

Our New Year celebrations burn bright but brief. Unaccustomed to all the excitement we peak too soon, finishing our limited alcohol well short of midnight, and at 9.30pm I am the last to crawl into my sleeping bag.

~

I am getting better at reading the river. I understand the curve of the water ahead and what it means for finding the right line.

Rounding a bend I see Mason loitering in the shallows against a pebble beach, still seated and fiddling with his spray deck. 'Are we stopping here for lunch?' I call out.

'I've already eaten. You guys can do what you want.' He pushes away from the shore without looking up and paddles off.

Right.

This atmosphere. This undefined, unspoken *thing* that has not been formally acknowledged but cannot be ignored. I hate it. I feel the tension rise in my throat, the constriction. It's Frank all over again.

I lived with it for years though I rarely challenged it, instead assuming I must have done something wrong. The eye rolls, the sighs, the huffing and puffing, but at what? I don't know why I never said anything.

But then one day something triggered in me, his actions so incongruent with love that finally even I could recognise the difference. We were on holiday. I stood next to our rental van after hoisting two kayaks to the roof. He tied his on first and then threw a rope to me and stood back, challenging me to tie my own on. 'I … I don't know how …' I stammered, confused. *Why didn't he just tie them both on? He always tied them on.* He sighed heavily, snatching the rope from me.

Nothing had led to this moment, no argument, no conflict. It was just always there. We drove on, the atmosphere tense. After half an hour I spoke.

'I think we might as well finish this. There doesn't seem to be any point continuing,' I said. He was silent and I took it as agreement, feeling a cloud lift. *Yes! Thank God for that! It's* over!

But then he spoke. 'It's my fault. You keep the van and I'll go stay in a hotel.'

'No, I don't care. It's fine. I'll go do my own thing. I mean, we've got this hiking permit booked together for next week but apart from that, there's nothing …' I trailed off, thinking practicalities.

I can't remember now how he did it but our 'break-up' lasted about half an hour.

He feigned fault.

I was glad, moving on.

But then softly, almost imperceptibly, he reeled me back in. Perhaps he sold it as the easier path. The *right* path. One that would now be different.

His persuasion. His expert soothing.

My indecision and lack of belief.

It was as though I had no control, swept along in the current just like I am on this river. He wouldn't let me go. I needed *him* to let me go.

~

The last 43 kilometres are tiring. The river widens and flattens and we paddle, now without the help of the river's current, into a headwind all the way to the river mouth, and waiting for us there with a van full of backpacks and boots is Ron. It's time to walk again.

The hard shoulder of State Highway 3 is vicious on my feet. Cars and trucks push funnels of air that nudge me sideways.

People complain about the road sections but I don't mind them too much. Any day where the trail actually has space for my head and feet to pass through, where I won't get ripped to shreds by foliage, and where there isn't a chance I might fall off the path and perhaps die is a good day in my books. Road is mileage that passes quickly. I can average five or six kilometres an hour on tarmac, more than double what I can cover in thick, hilly forests. It's all progress.

Antoine marches ahead, his jacket a black dot in the distance. I turn to see Isabel, our new German teammate, 300 metres behind me, and beyond her the tall khaki figure of Liam. Mason is nowhere to be seen. I'm glad. I can breathe again.

Isabel blends easily into our group. She is unobtrusive, seeming to listen more than she speaks. Each night she slinks away to dictate notes into her phone. I am sure we are fodder for her writing.

'I didn't come across many other hikers before I met you guys,' she tells me at day's end.

I study her, a woman seemingly unfazed by the act of walking alone, and wonder what her secret is. 'Do you take many rest days?'

'I haven't had a day off since I started.'

'*Whaaat?* That was like 1400 kilometres ago!'

'But I've had a few half days. That's like a day off.'

I'm glad to have some female company but also to boost the size of my team, my backup. Ahead of us lie the Tararua Ranges, the first of the serious mountains with intimidating elevation profiles and notorious wind. They're not to be taken lightly. In only the last few days, news has filtered through to us of a British hiker who perished in the Nelson Lakes section of trail, in the South Island, after falling off a cliff and landing in a glacial lake 180 metres below. Andy Wyatt was an experienced hiker with all the required gear, and search and rescue could only speculate as to what had happened. Was he blown off by a random gust of wind, disoriented in bad visibility, or was it a simple trip of a boot on the steep and rocky terrain? No one knows for sure. It strikes a sobering nerve.

7

Lessons from the Wild

*'This section includes many steep ascents
and descents. Weather in the Tararua Ranges
is notorious for deteriorating rapidly.
Be prepared for extreme conditions
at all times.'*

The trees and rocks are furry, like green flock. Beds of damp peat moss grow thick and deep, punctuated with leaves that bend in on themselves like curled green tongues drinking moisture from the mist. Every square inch is covered in life. It feels as though I'm walking through a living, breathing being.

I cross a stream and a man splashes past, clad in a t-shirt, running shorts and trail runners, clutching only a red plastic mug. Without stopping, he bends to scoop a cup of water, pouring it down his throat before disappearing into the ferns.

Rivers have become more frequent as we've travelled south and no longer do we need to carry much drinking water. I'm glad. My pack already bulges with nine days of food just in case the weather decides to hold us hostage.

I climb for hours, emerging without warning above the tree line into white mist and a blustery wind. A hut stands solid against this midsummer onslaught but its doorhandle is nearly yanked from my hand by a gust, dragging me across the slippery wet deck. Antoine and Isabel are already inside and halfway through lunch.

I pull a fleece and beanie from my pack and nod hello to a giant sitting in the corner – Dieter from Germany. He's already decided to stay the night.

The door opens again with a sudden howl of icy wind and Liam eases himself inside, flopping down on the bench seat next to me and looking unusually solemn. 'How do *you* feel?' he asks, puffs of condensation floating from his mouth.

'Yeah, all good. You?'

'I'm freezing.' His face is grim. 'I feel like I've walked a whole day already.'

'Oh?'

'I'll probably stay here the night,' he says.

'Really?' I'm surprised.

'Ah, I know me. I'm not going to feel better today.'

'Wow. Yeah? Well, we're not going to leave you on your own. Maybe you can walk on with Dieter and we'll meet you at the next hut, or further on. At least by the end of this section.'

Dieter nods.

'Okay.' Liam seems to have lost even the modest spark he usually shows.

Antoine, Isabel and I push on, climbing through low scrub fully exposed to the wind and spattering rain. Thick fog reduces the landscape to just the few metres around us but I feel charged, connected to the raw energy of the mountains that seem to buzz beneath me like a natural power station.

Back in the forest the trail rises and falls, a relentless roller-coaster. A small tree swings wildly in the wind, teetering as though struggling to take the weight of the growth on it. Hours of damp chill are starting to drain me and I'm relieved when the tin roof of a hut finally appears in the mist, leaking smoke from a chimney.

I hang my poles on the back deck before noticing another set propped in the corner. *Damn.* I pull my boots off and go inside.

'Hi Mason.'

He mumbles hello back, prodding the fireplace with a long stick, face buried close to its heavy iron door.

His irritation is palpable – a presence that spreads way beyond his physical being.

Great.

Silently I pledge not to engage, to separate myself from the tension. It feels like a challenge set for me, a lesson I must learn – to let others have their dramas if they choose but not take them on myself.

I'm deliberately perky with Antoine and Isabel. Making light. Laughing. Mason retreats to the sleeping quarters while the rest of us drag heavy vinyl-covered mattresses from the bedroom to the lounge and line them up in front of the fire. We toast marshmallows on sticks and lie bundled next to each other in our sleeping bags, mesmerised by the fire that crackles and pops. A warm glow spreads within and without. Somehow

I have managed to walk more than 1500 kilometres, halfway on this epic trail, and I am blessed to have found the company of new friends to share it with. I feel safe now. Secure. They won't leave me.

Outside the wind whistles and howls as I drift off to sleep, dreaming of better weather in the morning.

~

'What do you think?' Isabel murmurs in the dim early light.

Three faces peer through the draughty window, eyeing the shaking treetops glistening with moisture. 'I guess we're probably not going to really know until we get out there and have a look,' I say.

'Well, I don't want to stay here all day,' says Antoine.

Is this normal Tararua windy or dangerous windy? I study the notes of a route largely above the tree line, without shelter. '"Be prepared to wait out storms," it says.' I look out the window again. It's not exactly a storm. Perhaps it just sounds bad because of the wind whistling around the hut.

No one is keen to sit in a cold hut all day. Movement seems better. We can always turn around if it gets bad.

~

'Do you think we should turn around?' Isabel yells through the hood of her jacket, her voice instantly whisked away on the roaring wind. Antoine is fast disappearing in the white mist ahead, too far away to communicate with. I consider the trail we've just covered, a steady two-hour ascent to a rocky, exposed ridge. Somewhere ahead lies the shelter of the forest. Even if we did turn around now we'd still have to negotiate the same exposed ground.

'Nah, we'll be right!' I yell back, gesturing with my hand for her to move forward.

The wind that was manageable to start with now blows with violent force. The ridge narrows to a relative knife-edge and I stagger along it like a one-year-old learning to walk, arms and legs wide for balance. My backpack has turned me into a sail on legs, catching every random gust with maximum efficiency. I drop to hands and knees, clutching at rocks and tufts of grass.

For a moment the whiteout clears, revealing immense, dark treed valleys so far below it scares me. The white mist rolls and boils, flowing towards us and then, *whoosh*, solid white envelops us again.

The wind cranks to a new crazed intensity, screaming like a jet engine. It blows in my face, pushing air down my throat with such velocity I can't properly process it. My eyes stream, vision blurs. I no longer feel I'm hiking in New Zealand but rather that I've been nudged into a parallel universe where there are no rocks or grass around me, only a pure raging whiteness.

We shouldn't be here. I know it now but it's too late to plan an escape. The only way out is through. I crouch for whole minutes at a time, spreading my centre of gravity, vaguely aware of Antoine and Isabel nearby, hunched and gripping their poles with as much determination as me. Communication is not an option. We are each in our own private battle.

A violent gust slams me to the ground. I haul myself to my feet, readying to stagger a few more steps. Another gust slams me down. Pellets of rain sting like rubber bullets.

I push on, my bursts of forward movement gradually becoming more frequent. The wind is easing. A dark mass appears faintly in the mist. *Trees!* I strain towards them with all the desperation of a drowning person reaching for a life buoy.

Twisted and gnarled trunks wrap around me, ushering me into their safety. They've had years of weathering this abuse. They guide me down to Dracophyllum Hut, fireman orange with one set of bunk beds and barely enough room for the three of us to stand. We'll have to push on. I shiver and shake through lunch, shovelling crackers, pesto and chocolate into my mouth like a coal stoker on a steam train, and then head back out.

Boulders, ladders of tree roots, knee-jarring descents. I slip on mud and wrap myself around a tree, legs straddling each side of its trunk and one foot dangling in midair. I wrestle to get back on my feet, cursing the tree until it occurs to me that the immovable column has likely arrested my fall down a bottomless ravine.

I'm tired, growing grumpier by the moment. The wind has stolen precious energy with its pushing and shoving. Small wisps of hair escape my braids and tickle my nose, which runs like a tap.

A faint beep emanates from the front pocket of my pack.

'Message from Liam. He says he's leaving tomorrow with Dieter and Lance.'

'When did he send it?' Isabel asks.

'I don't know whether he sent it just now or I only just got coverage —'

'Where is he now?' Antoine butts in.

'Is he feeling better?' says Isabel.

'Who's Lance?' Antoine again.

Suddenly I feel confused. 'Ahh, I don't know.' I wish everyone would slow down a bit. My lips stumble over the words, slurring. Shit. Exhaustion and cold have dulled my mind. I quietly mention it to Isabel and she shifts position to walk behind me.

Above the tree line once again, and in thick fog, our faint trail withers to nothing, lost amongst a tumble of grey rocks. I compare map and GPS, frowning intently from one to the other, the cogs turning more slowly than ever. Antoine dashes in different directions, searching for clues, while Isabel quietly studies the trail notes. 'How about down this way?' She points to a wall of mist that looks the same as every other direction and Antoine disappears over the lip of the ridge to investigate. 'Yes, there is a rock cairn down here!'

Nichols Hut is perched just above the tree line — six mattresses squeezed over two sleeping platforms. Wet clothes hang from wires strung from the ceiling and the last embers of a fire burn in the stove, tended by an American couple.

'We tried to head out this morning,' says Joe. 'Walked up the ridge to have a look but it was too crazy so we came back here.'

'Smart move. We just about got blown off the top.' I still feel shaken.

A hot chickpea curry thaws me from the inside and then I climb into the warmth of my sleeping bag, tired muscles tingling with relief at being off duty for the night. It took us an exhausting nine hours to cover just 13 kilometres – a new record for slow.

Outside the wind howls like a monster that might drag us off into oblivion if one of us should venture outside. *What the hell am I doing out here? I should be reclining in a hot bath with a glass of wine, a pizza and a little fluffy dog by my side.* I long for the creature comforts that make me feel normal and safe. The music from my earphones helps, but there is no escaping the fact that I'm on the top of the middle of nowhere and only I will be able to get myself out – tomorrow, or the next day. Night-time is just an interval.

~

I wake to find the Americans quietly stuffing their backpacks, readying to go in beanies and jackets. Blue sky peeks through a window blurred with condensation, though the wind still howls. I snuggle deeper into my bag, in no hurry to leave its warmth.

The call of nature eventually forces me outside and the view that was hidden the day before is sudden and dazzling. I sit on the loo with the door open, breathing in the pure cold air. Mottled green mountains roll far into the distance, unmarred by signs of civilisation and shot with long, misted beams from the rising sun. *This is why I'm out here!* Yes, the mountains hold danger, but now I see their beauty too.

Forty-five minutes pass and Joe and Liz do not return. The wind must be manageable up on the ridge. I'm not sure whether to be relieved or disappointed. I pull a beanie over my head and follow Antoine and Isabel back up to the main trail and, free of its veil of white mist, I can actually *see* the mighty Tararua Range. Thick, bottle-green foliage gives way at the tree line to tussock littered with craggy nubs of granite. Rock falls scatter the steep mountainsides, and here and there the earth shows scars from landslips. The ranges seem dynamic and powerful, their sheer size and untamed wildness intimidating.

Antoine hurries into the distance, face hidden within his storm hood. His hands are clad in thick white rubber gloves, bought on the cheap at the last minute to protect against the biting wind, giving him the appearance of a mad surgeon. Behind him by 100 metres is Isabel, and I follow at the rear.

We track over summits and knobs, the fog coming and going, flashing glimpses of mountains and the distant Tasman Sea. I tread down narrow rutted tracks gingerly and climb on all fours over rocky outcrops, all the while fearing slipping off the back of this great beast.

The flat light grows, building to something resembling sunshine, and an easy ridge-top path spreads out before us, well into the distance. With a grin I dare to hope that the hardest of the Tararuas may be behind us.

My feet fairly skip across the trail but still I stop regularly to marvel at the views and take photos, and every time I do the rest of my team gains considerable ground, but today I refuse to rush. It's simply too beautiful. *Does it look best from here? Actually, maybe 50 metres on would be better.* Camera out, camera away. Isabel pauses, waiting for me to catch up.

'All good?' she asks.

'How amazing is this!' I gush.

She smiles. 'Sounds like you're enjoying it.'

I stop to pull some washing from my pack, tying it to the outside, and the distance between us grows again.

The tree line looms. Antoine and Isabel stop just shy of the forest, waiting for me.

'You are slow today. What is wrong?' Antoine asks brusquely.

'Nothing ... I ...' I trail off, surprised at the question. 'I've just been enjoying the scenery. Stopped a few times –'

He turns before I can finish, disappearing down into the trees and my joy is suddenly clipped. *I don't* want *to rush!* I want to yell after him.

But he's gone.

Slow. 'What is slow anyway?' I grizzle to myself. Our pace already falls well within the estimated walking times. No one is nudging to do any more kilometres in a day than we do already so where is the harm in taking time to enjoy it? We don't *need* to rush!

My annoyance is brief, overrun by feelings of delicacy. It's Frank again. He is reflecting back at me from everywhere. The rushing, the drama he loved, problems created from nothing. *Why? Why?* I can't tolerate another moment of it.

I descend through steep forest but the wind has gone from my sails. Half an hour passes. Down, down. My knees grumble. Isabel is creeping ahead again, Antoine out of sight. I try to go faster but my foot lands on a green rock, scraping off a layer of moss as I slide, the full weight of my body and pack landing heavily on another rock. I roll sideways off it, gasping at the sudden white heat bursting across my rump.

'Are you okay?' Isabel rushes back.

The pain has stolen my voice. I lie on my side in the black dirt for minutes, wincing, trying to breathe through it. I ease myself to my feet and gently put weight on my left leg, testing it for function. 'Okay,' I finally whisper.

Every step twists and pulls at my left butt cheek, the swelling around my muscles making it feel as though a tennis ball has merged with them. The fall felt like a slap, an urging to wake up and tighten my game, but I'm tired and barely half an hour later my feet slip out from under me again. I bounce on my backside and then topple head first, the weight of my pack pushing me forward. Time slows down. Flashes of earth, flying sunglasses, walking poles. Fragrant dirt up my nose. *Which way is up?* I keep bouncing.

Eventually it stops.

'Are you alright? Don't move!' Panicked, Isabel edges her way down to me as quickly as she dares.

'I'm okay.' I respond brightly, automatically, before I've had a chance to do a full stocktake. I inspect my arms and hands, ingrained with dirt. My whole body has been rolled in it but mercifully I can't feel any new aches and pains.

'Are you sure? You fell quite a way.' Isabel crouches beside me, unconvinced.

Shaking with adrenalin, I sit on a log to wait for the shivering to subside and the cumulative exhaustion that I had only just managed to forget about rushes back to consciousness. For seventy-two days I have been walking, having perhaps one day off a week. They've been long days, hard days. If I'd been travelling alone I would have chosen more rest but I have been keeping pace with the others for company, for security. My body wants a break though, and rushing only seems to be making things worse.

Waitewaewae Hut appears at noon like a welcoming rainforest retreat, modern and spacious, nestled amongst ferns dappled in sunlight that filters through the canopy. Water tinkles over river stones nearby, sounding like a day-spa water feature. I *need* to stay here.

'Liam's still behind us, anyway; there's no need to push on. And this place is lovely.' I dump my pack on the deck.

Antoine feels the same, though Isabel is less convinced, reluctant to let a half-day pass. Finally there is unanimous agreement to stay and I drag a mattress onto the deck to collapse in the sun's healing warmth. Lying down, the 'tennis ball' under my skin feels even more noticeable and my knees hurt. My body aches so much I can't bear to move.

Afternoon turns to evening and the air quickly cools. Antoine lights a match in the fireplace and I pick up a newspaper, left behind as a fire starter, turning the pages absentmindedly until a full-page advertisement leaps out. *A Massive 30–50% Off!* Fat red and black fonts, prices with dramatic slashes across them – it reads like a message from another world. I stare at it, feeling strangely rocked, as though an unruly passenger has just invaded my rowboat on a peaceful lake. It takes a few moments to regain equilibrium.

That's right, I think, *this is normal.* I recall department stores, shopping centres, acres of stuff waiting to be bought, bright lights, piped music, sales, buying just for the hell of it. My brain falters, retrieving memories from another life. The concept seems insanely foreign. For two and a half months I've happily existed with just 11 kilograms of belongings. I could list every item I currently 'own' off the top of my head. There is not one that I don't regularly use nor is there anything I want for.

I realise just how distanced from society I have become. The ad that would once have seemed so normal, just background noise skimmed over without a thought, now seems very odd, disturbing even. Part of a spell, a hypnosis I have broken free from. I don't *need* extra stuff in my life. Having less has made my life a whole lot simpler.

I throw the paper back in the box and crawl into my sleeping bag.

My body is tired and sore but I'm *happy*. I'm glad I'm out here with just my one bag of things. I feel alive. I've done something with my body, used it actively, as it was designed.

A gentle breeze nudges the hut, rustling the trees, and behind that, even fainter, the sound of the river – nature wrapping around us.

~

Two days later we descend to the sleepy town of Waikanae. After the untamed Tararuas, the sight of clean, well-fed people walking dogs past neat flowerbeds seems noticeably odd.

Reunited with Liam and Dieter, we walk the Kapiti Coast, sun-drenched against a twinkling flat sea, and at the safety of sea level I begin to see joy in the traverse behind us. Despite its dangers, part of me enjoyed the power and ruthlessness of the elements. The mountain's complete disregard for us, or awareness of our existence, flung me into unfamiliar territory. I was no longer cocooned, protected by the many safety nets modern life provides. Perhaps the challenging conditions reminded me of how humans used to exist – they were unsafe, vulnerable, but living, for *real*. Wild. This is a place where humans are not central.

~

At the bottom of the North Island, Wellington looms. The nation's capital.

I could have been a New Zealander. My parents grew up in the well-to-do countryside south of London, in the thick of World War II. As children they had held their mothers' hands under staircases as the bombs fell. Everyone had a gas mask, my mother's teddy bear included. My parents married when Mum was twenty-one and Dad was twenty-three, and barely four months later they set sail for Australia. The Australian government had offered a deal – commit to stay and work for at least two years and we'll transport you across the world for only ten pounds. New Zealand and Canada were taking on newcomers too, but in the end my parents chose Australia. It was supposed to be an adventure, a journey that would eventually end with their return to the motherland.

Before long though, my brother came along and suddenly we were all committed. Two years later my sister arrived and six years after that, when my parents had all but given up, I reluctantly followed.

I'm glad we stayed in Oz. The land suited our lifestyle, with plenty of space and a climate that encouraged exploring the great outdoors. We all enjoyed it. I was probably eight when we began the ritual of a Sunday barbecue followed by a bushwalk, often in the damp fern-filled gullies of the Dandenong Ranges. Afterwards Mum would cook a roast while I wrestled with my brother on the living-room carpet. Most of the time he'd let me win but sometimes he'd pin me down, my eight-year-old efforts no match for his sixteen-year-old body. Once he hung my sister from a doorknob, the tights under her jeans tied in a knot at her feet and slung over the handle. She dangled helplessly, turning beet red, tears of laughter streaming down her face while the rest of us cheered on.

Under a hot Australian sun we played hide-and-seek or swam in the backyard pool my father had dug. My brother and sister charged around its vinyl-covered circular walls so fast that whirlpools formed and I simply floated on my back, carried by their efforts as the gum trees whizzed by overhead.

I don't know what happened but at some point our universe expanded. In some great cosmic explosion we suddenly floated outwards to our own corners of the galaxy – Mum back to work, Dad to his shed, my brother out of the family home and my sister to adulthood and the boyfriends that went with it. Everyone had things to do, places to be. Everyone except me.

There was a sudden void in my world, a pushing of distance between us. I discovered if there's one way to really piss your older sister off it's to wear the same t-shirt as her. Dad kept occupied with projects – the construction of furniture or the moulding of a kayak. 'Why don't you go play on the freeway,' he liked to joke when I tugged on his sleeve. When I saw my mother put on her long dress in the evenings, off to play host at wedding receptions, I howled. I howled even more when I didn't see her do it. Suddenly she was just gone and I'd realise I was alone.

In my mother's absence I saw more of my grandmother, who had also emigrated, and between games of gin rummy she educated me on the finer points of ironing handkerchiefs to perfection and how to be a good guest. 'You come from good stock, you do!' she said, wagging a finger and holding my gaze to drive home the point. It was important that I did things right.

In this altered world, my closest friend was Killer. He was quiet and loving and sat sagely on my bed, all fluffy paws and golden flyaway hair. He'd started off as Sparky but within a week Dad thought 'Killer' might suit the little silky terrier better. That was Dad's sense of humour.

You can never feel too alone with a dog. They are always there for you, always happy to cuddle and share a moment. A dog will never roll its eyes at you or tell you you're a pain in the arse. It'll never pick you last for the team. I think dogs have been my best friends ever since. That seems pretty sad now.

~

Wellington is our halfway point but to get there we must cross the open grassy flanks of Mount Kaukau. Wind funnels between the nearby Cook Strait, which divides North and South islands, the air rushing powerfully like an incoming tide, and again I am battered by it.

As the metropolis comes into view so do the lycra-clad city folk loitering at a lookout. I'm in disbelief. Surely this isn't weather to face voluntarily. I cross paths with a couple out for a Sunday walk. 'Is this normal?' I yell into the buffeting wind, staggering to stay put. My voice evaporates, carried off by the wind monster, but they seem to know what I'm saying.

'Oh, yes, Wellington is known for being windy.'

'How are you doing that?' I yell back, gesturing at them: they're almost completely stationary, with hands casually slotted into hip pockets. It's as though they're in a bubble. I think they're laughing because their mouths are open and their eyes crinkle but I can't hear anything other than the roaring wind. I risk lifting a hand from my supporting hiking pole to wave goodbye and stagger on.

Two hours later the glass doors of a hotel slide closed behind me and for the first time all day the air is silent and still. The lobby mirror reflects a slightly crazed-looking woman with frizzy hair. The TV weatherman informs me the wind was gusting at 70 kilometres per hour.

~

The breakfast buffet is bountiful. Fresh fruit, croissants, steaming scrambled eggs, crispy bacon, roasted potatoes and tomatoes – it seems I have never known such abundance. I fall into a faux-leather chair and marvel at its padded comfort. Outside, the trees still lean and shake violently but I eat my fill and head out into it.

It's 15 kilometres to the sea, to the end of the North Island, and by chance Antoine, Isabel and I scoop up Joe, Liz and Dieter on the way, our friends from the Tararuas. Liam is satisfied with having reached a hostel in the city. For him, the North Island is done.

We walk to the coast and with reverence each of us touches a rock embedded with a plaque – 1620 kilometres walked so far, it says, and 1430 yet to go. I let my fingers wander over the bronze, trying to *feel* the distance the words say I've walked. I think back to the start, to Cape Reinga more than two months ago, when so much of the future was uncertain. The reality of what hiking every day might be like, the fear of the unknown, of what lay ahead, of walking alone. But somehow it's worked out. I've made it halfway, and if I can do one half then surely I can do the other half too?

Antoine pulls a bottle of champagne from his backpack and I smile fondly at him. Trust a Parisian to pack a bottle of champers on a day hike. The pop of the cork breaks our reverence, releasing whoops of celebration. Antoine takes the first swig before handing it to me and I pour the bubbles down my throat like a Formula One race driver on the podium. We flop into the grass, drinking and snacking on Pringles while chattering about forward plans, fatiguing gear and injuries. But as the conversation continues, my own thoughts start to drift away, drifting south.

South. The land of innumerable river crossings, of high and inhospitable alpine peaks and saddles. The land of exposed mountainsides, of cold and possibly snow, of route-standard trail with no definable track to follow. Where I'll need my nascent navigation skills, and the trail is 'not quite mountaineering'. Whatever we have achieved so far suddenly seems just a warm-up for what is to come. Maybe I got through the north by luck. The Tararuas certainly taught me a lesson or two but the south is where I will truly be tested.

At least I am no longer alone. Antoine will pull away from the trail in a few weeks' time, his holiday coming to an end, but I've still got Isabel and Liam and it feels like a good team. We walk at the same pace, we get on and we're all heading the same way.

Just keep going, Laura. Give it a go. See how far you can get.

~

Hiker party in Wellington in two days. Spread the word. A message appears on the Te Araroa Facebook page.

'Ooh, a party!' I glance from the computer to Isabel.

'It says here Kiwi Scout is coming,' she says, flicking through her phone.

'Excellent!'

Kiwi Scout has taken on an almost legendary status in our minds, a New Zealander who has already completed the entire trail. So few hikers have done it that anyone who has survived it is of great interest, and we've been avidly following his blogs and posts to glean precious tips.

'Steve and Brad reckon they're going to put in an all-nighter to get here in time.'

'What? Those guys are crazy. I'd never walk at night,' I say, but inside the butterflies flutter gently. After walking the same track for months without crossing paths, I will finally see Steve again. I comb my fingers through my hair in the mirror and wonder how I'm going to make myself look any tidier in my one hiking outfit.

I've been a long time in the wilds. A bit of city action will be fun.

~

A dozen-odd heavily bearded and tanned faces gather in the corner of the pub, buzzing with tales of adventure. There are only a few I don't know. I meet Lance, six foot something and blonde, walking straight off the trail and into the pub in short shorts, long t-shirt, clumpy boots and a brown beanie. He's an imposing man with a sure voice, walking to raise awareness of the degradation of New Zealand's waterways. Rivers are being drained to irrigate farms, leaving habitats drying and dying, he tells me. Their waters are being polluted from the leeching of fertilisers and animal waste, making them dangerous to native plants and animals. It seems all may not be as pristine as I thought.

I wander the room, chatting to people – *my* people. Long-distance hiking is so different and all-consuming it's difficult to fully convey our lives – our challenges, sufferings and joys – to someone who hasn't experienced the same path.

I scan the room for two more faces but they're not here.

'You look like your glass is nearly empty, can I get you a

drink?' A man with a bushy dark beard suddenly appears beside me, smiling warmly. 'I'm Pat, or Kiwi Scout.'

'Hi!' I take a gulp of champagne to slow the questions queuing for attention, and manage a bit of small talk before launching in.

'So what are the Richmond Ranges like? It sounds pretty gnarly from the trail notes.'

'Oh, they're not too bad. Just take your time.'

'And the Waiau Pass? How was that? The guidebook says something about it being not quite mountaineering and I know if a Kiwi says that then it's pretty freaking close.'

He laughs. 'Yeah, look, you'll be fine, just make sure the weather is good. Wait it out if you have to. You'll be okay.'

I feel reassured by his words and his calm, authoritative voice. Then he blows it all by saying he works for the armed forces. He's probably tough as hell.

But he *does* think I can do it. I try to focus on the positive.

Kiwi Scout moves on to share his wisdom with others and another hour passes. I wander back to the bar and, from behind, a voice speaks. 'Hey, Laura.'

I turn to see a familiar smile. 'Steve!' I fling my arms around him for a long squeeze.

'It's good to see you!' He pulls away, looking into my face. 'You look really hot,' he smiles shyly before adding, 'Really fit, too. Strong, I mean.' He braces his arms in front of him like a body builder.

'Yeah, well, I've been working out. You look good too. You look hairier!' I laugh, tugging at a new rusty beard.

We pause, studying each other, the seven weeks apart having changed us in ways more than physical.

'I've *missed* you,' he says, voice quieter. 'What happened to you after Auckland? I thought we'd see you again.'

'Yeah, I thought I'd bump into you sooner too, but you guys went to visit friends and family and … I guess it just didn't work out …'

Away from the bar I lose him to the group – voices talking and laughing across the table. I sneak glances, trying to get used to his beard, remembering the enthusiasm he gives to every conversation. The free laugh, the bouncing Tigger-like body.

Alcohol seeps into our lean bodies with maximum impact, the mood growing more raucous by the hour. All eyes have an extra-glassy sparkle to them and a few start to droop slightly. Somewhere in the fog of alcohol and tiredness Steve and I find each other again and in a darkened corner we kiss. He's shy at first, tentative, mouth tainted with cigarette smoke. 'I thought you'd given up,' I whisper.

He turns away, grimacing. 'Ahh, that probably didn't taste too good.' He looks back again, eyebrows raised.

'Oh, I don't know. Try it again.'

The smoke is foul but I don't care, driven only by the months of wondering and the urge to be close to someone. I feel the heat of his body, a kind and good man who reached out to me when I was in need and alone. A man who made sure I never fell too far behind. I've studied the curls of his hair, his freckled cheeks, his broad shoulders. I've trailed the line of his lips in my mind and wondered what they would be like to kiss. Now I know. Smoky. But nice.

The group moves as a herd to a club a block away, dancing under a flashing pulse of red light, a melee of arms and legs, punching the air, twirling around. I work my way across to Steve but he's talking with others, laughing, yelling into Summer's ear about something. I retreat, philosophical, enjoying the moment for what it is – friends, music, alcohol, talking, dancing. Not hiking. Only Liam looks awkward, shuffling from left to right, shaking closed fists by his sides. There's a smile on his face but he yells into my ear, 'I'd rather be alone in the bush.'

At midnight Steve is nowhere to be found so I slink away with Isabel and it's only once we're on the streets that my phone rings. 'Hey, where are you?' he asks.

'On our way home. Sorry, we couldn't find you.'

'I was hoping we could spend some time together.'

'Next time,' I say.

~

I escape from the excesses of the night unscathed. I wake thinking of Steve, satisfied my itch has been scratched, wondering what he is thinking. I think about the kiss that went nowhere. But only a little.

'Liam seemed a bit distant last night,' I mumble to Isabel, stretched out on the bed opposite.

'Oh, I had a chat to him. He was wondering why we haven't booked on the same ferry as him to the South Island.'

'But he booked before us! He didn't even discuss it.'

'Apparently he was worried that we might not be walking with him. He doesn't want to be on his own down south.'

At least we're all still on the same page on that.

8

South

Ship Cove feels like the tropics, a tangle of greenery floating down the hillside to meet a crystal-clear bay ringing with the trill of cicadas and birdsong. Dolphins guided our water taxi here. Not a single cloud mars the blue sky and, sheltered from the wind, the air is almost warm. It's not what I expected the South Island to be.

Beyond two carved Māori totems, Isabel and I find Steve and Brad leaning against their packs in the grass. Brad's preoccupied with his blossoming moustache, twirling it with newly purchased wax into impressive upturned curls, the distinguished facial hair at odds with the rest of him. Steve smiles at me, a quick wink, almost imperceptible, but his hands fiddle with the rolling of tobacco, triggering in me a surge of desire and revulsion that cancel each other out.

'Well … I guess we'll see you guys later on, then.' I adjust my pack and leave them to follow Isabel on a long climb to a ridge. Three days of easy walking await us, with stunning sea views over Queen Charlotte Sound, and I'm excited at the prospect.

The conditions are perfect and I can look forward to knocking off another 70 kilometres without fear of navigational challenges or mortal injury.

Three days off in Wellington, combined with a massage and plenty of good food, have revived me, and after months of hiking my body is now stronger and fitter than it's ever been. Walking with poles and a backpack is a full-body workout and it dawns on me that I'd rather spend eight hours on a trail than one hour in a gym.

In the city the gym was my only real choice but I never liked its sticky air and smell of stale sweat. It was full of people in brightly coloured clothes with slogans stretched across their chests like 'NEVER. GIVE. UP.' People who groaned through gritted teeth under the weight of kettle bells and medicine balls, sometimes literally roaring with the effort. It all seemed to have an air of self-flagellation about it to me, ceding to a culture that tells us we're lacking somehow. And if you believe that then you set yourself up for all sorts of trouble.

I wonder if we'd still go to the gym if no one was watching – the last person on the planet perhaps. If there were no one there to witness us afterwards, to see if we'd grown leaner or firmer, would we do it then?

I'd like a t-shirt that says 'Be kind to yourself'.

~

It's nearly seven o'clock when we reach Camp Bay. A ranger greets us, mentioning a waterside bar a five-minute walk away. Isabel and

I glance at each other in silent agreement. He shifts to leave then turns again. 'Oh, and ah, has anyone told you about the weka?'

I've seen a few of these characters already – flightless brown birds the size of a small chicken loitering around picnic tables.

'Just be careful with your belongings. They sometimes steal stuff from around your tent, even from under the flysheet.'

I pick a site close to the water, scanning for weka and munching on a chocolate bar while I set up camp. I take a few bites and then rest the bar on my pack while I slot the tent poles together, but there is a sudden flash of movement and the pink and gold of the wrapper disappears into the bush on two furiously running brown legs. 'Nooooo!' I reach out but it's gone. 'Lucky that block was nearly finished anyway,' I grumble.

'Don't worry. Let's get these tents up and go get a drink, hey?'

The bar is a homely deck over the water, fringed with lanterns. Next to it we find Liam and Antoine dangling fishing lines off the edge of a wooden jetty. Antoine is beside himself. 'We just saw a killer whale!'

'No *way!*' *A killer whale? Here? Just a moment ago?* I scan the water, desperate to find it.

'Yes, he was right underneath the jetty. I just heard him. He came up for air right under us!'

Though I haven't seen it, the mere thought that one is in the vicinity adds further magic to the place, in a region that has been nothing but beautiful since we arrived.

Long shadows stretch across the distant mountains as the cold sauvignon blanc slides down my throat. I zip the neck of my fleece higher against the cooling air, taking in the view, and suddenly there they are – unmistakably huge dorsal fins slowly piercing the surface. 'Look!' I leap to my feet, pointing.

The barman hurries past to a rubber inflatable dinghy tied to the jetty, beckoning us aboard. We speed across the water, cutting the engine to drift within viewing distance without crowding them. The glossy black bodies arc through the water and the air is filled with their misty exhalations. They move slowly but their strength is clear.

I become aware of time slowing down, everything else falling away, leaving just this moment of power and grace and purity. I feel my body surrender to it, all other thoughts fading. I drift with nature as it reveals itself to me, drifting with life as it unfolds. You can never know when these moments might surface – they can't be planned for – but magic like this happens, usually when you least expect it.

The lesson seems to be: loosen your grip on what you *think* life is and you make way for new possibilities, ones that might yield something beyond imagination. Already the South Island is revealing itself to be more than I expected.

The sky is pitch black when we stagger down the short track to our tents. I wonder how anything could top such an incredible day when I notice the edge of the path lined with the pale glow of thousands of tiny green dots. Glow-worms.

~

The track passes through two working farms …
Farm operations and stock have right of way.
Potential hazards: electric fences.

The South Island's gentle welcome ebbs as its biggest challenge looms. The trail notes say the Richmond Ranges are suitable only for 'fit, experienced, and well-equipped trampers'. I wonder if I am now one of them.

The weather in the mountains is notoriously unstable but the forecast is good. I kneel on a small patch of grass outside a supermarket, sorting my food for the nine days ahead. It seems an obscene amount. My chocolate and nut quota alone is over a kilo and a half.

'Is there anything you want to leave with me?' Steve hovers over my mess. A phone call moments earlier has summoned him home for a brief visit, a family matter. 'I can store something for you until later if you want.'

'Nah, it's cool. Thanks.'

I've barely seen him in three days, our schedules mismatching – his late starts, my early finishes. Others have surrounded us. Nothing has been said about Wellington, about the kiss, and in the absence of any follow-up I'm swamped with self-consciousness, awkward and unsure, desperate not to be left alone with him. Liam, Antoine and Brad are still in the supermarket. Isabel gathers her empty packaging, preparing to head down the street to the bin. *Don't go!*

'Got any rubbish?' She walks away.

I busy myself stuffing food into nooks and crannies in my pack, the blood rushing in my ears.

'I should be back on the trail in a week,' he says. 'Where do you think you'll be by then?' He looks preoccupied, the cogs whirring.

'Oh, I don't know,' I say vaguely, shoving and poking at my pack, unable to meet his gaze.

'I'll get back on the trail as quick as I can. I'll walk fast to catch up.'

'Cool.' I keep packing.

~

Liam and Antoine hitch directly to the trailhead, missing the 30 kilometres of highway and farm pasture before it. Isabel and I walk it at our own pace, slowly drifting apart, and I enjoy the time alone and the extra freedoms it brings – my speed, my breaks, my terms.

Cow hooves have pressed deep potholes in the thick grass. At the top of a stile I hug a post for support, feeling a sudden and vicious twinge on the back of my leg. I yelp in pain and surprise, momentarily confused, then realise it was an electric shock – my third of the hike so far. Damn these farm fences. The field is full of cows, most gathered around another distant stile to be crossed. They're enormous, every one of their heads turned to stare blankly at me. Unnerved, I tiptoe through them, cooing quietly, uncertain if the soothing sounds are for their benefit or mine. '*Oookay* … I'm *juuust* going to walk through here … all right … there we go …'

From atop the next stile I assess the huge field ahead, empty save for a large black blob in its middle. I study it cautiously, wondering whether it's a rock, a pile of old tyres, or … a bull? I wince at the possibility.

I move quickly, hugging the fence line, but at halfway the black blob lifts his huge head and my heart contracts. *Shit!* I move quietly now, trying to become one with the grass. I risk a sideways glance, not wanting to challenge him with a full-frontal look, but he stays reclined. Death by electric shock or death by goring? I decide I will commando-roll under the fence if it comes to it.

Mercifully the bull remains uninspired by my passage and I finish the last of the farm-animal gauntlet, arriving at Pelorus Bridge to find Isabel munching on a muesli bar. 'How did you go with those cows?' I ask her. 'And the bull!'

'I got an electric shock on my head.'

'What? Are you okay?'

'Yes. I tried to walk under the fence,' she said. 'Everything went black for a moment. But I'm okay now.'

'Geez, well, take it easy!'

I pull a muffin from my pack then hesitate. 'I've got to cut back on my food a bit. I ate so much in Wellington and with the easy hiking in the last few days I can feel my pants ...' I tug at my waistband. 'Not so loose now.'

Isabel frowns at me. 'Laura, have you ever had an eating disorder?'

The question takes me by surprise. *Have I?* 'Um, I don't think so. I mean, I lost a lot of weight when I was in high school ...' I trail off, recalling the time. Twelve kilos in two months. I basically starved myself. I couldn't look at a plate of food without mentally calculating the calories on it, erring on overestimating just in case. Did that count as an eating disorder? From the clothes that remained of that time I was obviously a waif, though I didn't see it that way then. Like many other girls my age, I compared myself to the bodies in magazines and movies, criticising myself for not looking the same. I pored over articles that outlined diet plans, exercises that would make my tummy flatter, my butt firmer, ways to keep my boyfriend happy – the one I didn't yet have.

But things have been pretty normal since then. I think.

It took nearly a decade to loosen my grip on the calorie counting. I started eating peanut butter again. I ate enough to avoid the hunger. I allowed my weight to fluctuate gently with the seasons, accepting that though I might grow a winter coat in the cooler months I would shed it again without effort in the summer. I started to be kinder to myself, to love myself just a little more.

But then Frank came along, bringing a food obsession of his own.

It started on a road trip three months in – our first holiday together over the Christmas break. We pulled over to grab takeaway for dinner and I ordered spaghetti carbonara while he bought a kebab. We drove on, the hot plastic containers warming my lap as we searched for a park in which to eat, and I noticed that he'd gone quiet. What was up? Did I say something? I reran our conversation in my head.

'What's wrong?'

'Nothing.' His tone was quiet and dismissive as he stared through the windscreen.

It dawned on me later – I shouldn't have ordered the creamy sauce. Months later he dished up a chicken korma – a big plate of rice and curry for him and one lonely dollop of curry sauce for me.

'Where's my rice?' I asked.

'Oh, sorry! I thought you said you didn't *want* rice.' He recovered quickly, adding two small scoops of carbs.

Then there was the whole batch of jam tarts he gobbled minutes after I'd baked them. I returned to the kitchen to sample the fruits of my labour but could find only crumbs. 'Oh, sorry! I thought you said you didn't *want* any!' he gushed with a kind of exaggerated dismay. I was pissed. But I was curious too. His statements were patently untrue but did he actually believe what he was saying? I was never sure.

As someone so obsessed with his own body, he must have hated himself for eating all that fat and sugar. But I guess he thought it was better than me eating it.

Isabel and I camp in a small clearing beside Emerald Pool. I strip off by the water to wash then study my body. Muffins aside, it's undeniably leaner and firmer than it used to be. I barely have to flex to feel the muscles across my pelvis, in my arms, my legs, my bum. Even my 44-year-old boobs look reasonably pert thanks to the cold water. Only my skin has suffered, with small patches the texture of crepe paper on my shoulders and hips from the rubbing of my pack.

Naked, I lie on the hot rocks to dry. I rub my eyes vigorously, enjoying the satisfying tingle of blood flow behind them. There's no makeup to worry about spoiling; it's just me now, pure as the day I was born. Me and my one outfit drying in the sun. Me, washing in a river, gathering drinking water.

Simple. Happy. Me.

~

We find Liam and Antoine lazing outside a hut on the river, waiting for us. Reunited again, a team of four. Balance returned.

But the next day Antoine suddenly leaves us. I thought we still had another week to go but I am mistaken and his announcement over lunch that this is where we part, that in this moment we must say goodbye, panics me. I'm not ready! I haven't mentally prepared. The 1200 kilometres we have walked together: fifty-six days of fun, torture and everything in between. We've faced so much, done nearly everything together, yet now he will return to Paris and I can't imagine our paths will ever cross again.

He says he is ready to go – his knees are sore, his skin suffering, his body yearning for better nutrition.

I think of his quick smile, endless energy and humour – we are losing a cornerstone. Blinking back tears we embrace, thanking each other for everything we have shared. He looks a lonely figure walking away on his own. Poles clicking on the rocks, he turns to wave at us one last time before the forest swallows him up.

And now there are three.

~

The Richmond Alpine Track is rugged. The summits are consistently above 1500 metres and the track has many steep, exposed sections and stream crossings. It's only suitable for fit, experienced, and well-equipped trampers.

We leave early, climbing steeply to gain 900 metres in elevation. Step, pole plant, breathe, step, breathe, haul.

I emerge above the tree line onto an open gravel plateau in sight of Starveall Hut and the mountains that roll into the distance. Scree slopes, craggy grey rock pushing through dense dark forest: I soak it up, my heart soaring.

'Andy Wyatt wrote in the visitor book.' Isabel's voice floats from inside the hut. The man we read about in the news, the hiker who fell.

'What did he say?'

'Not too much. Just sounds like he was enjoying the hike.'

I join her inside and goose bumps ripple over my skin as I see the ink left, just over a month ago, by the Brit. Though we've never met I feel a connection. He was a Te Araroa hiker, just like us, on the adventure of a lifetime with no idea that his days were numbered. It would have been only a few weeks after leaving here that he fell to his death. My heart wrenches for his poor family.

This land takes no prisoners. The mistakes I made in the Tararuas – the tired, clumsy falls – they *cannot* happen here.

Above the tree line sparse orange marker poles replace the plastic orange triangles, guiding us over rocky scree and along a ridge that climbs, descends and climbs again. It's steep. Narrow ledges float above huge drops and I purposefully slow down. I've been walking eight hours. This is the hour of stumbling and tripping over boots.

The last stretch is pure steep descent, jarring my already painful knees, and I curse the fact that we've chosen a hut whose icon on the map is one contour-line-filled square – one kilometre of punishing steepness – away from the main trail. Old Man Hut sits in a flat, grassy clearing – five bunk beds and a fireplace. I carry a pot of cold water into the trees to wash, and steam rises from my body. It's colder than I realised. In the diminishing light a bank of cloud pours over the range, rolling towards us like a river of dry ice. Mount Rintoul towers over us – tomorrow's objective and the most difficult section of the Richmond Ranges, with lots of scrambling on exposed rock. I hate exposure. I've frozen on ledges more than once over the years, paralysed by the perilous drop beneath me, the possibility that a foot might slip and there I would go.

Just take it as it comes, Laura. Be brave.

Try.

The Pommy Improver Award – that's what they gave me at high-school ski camp. I feared the slopes, cursed my unwieldy skis and poles, which seemed to slide in every direction except the one I wanted. I blamed the fog that blinded me. I howled that I couldn't do it. But by the end of the week I had done it – fairly well. I think the teachers were sick of me complaining like a so-called whingeing Pom, but in the end everyone was happy, most of all me.

Twenty years later I found myself snowboarding in a whiteout, the edge of the run not quite where I expected it to be. Suddenly the ground gave way and the lip that I'd expected to be knee deep was actually well over my head. For the briefest of moments I landed it, my board secure on the snow, body miraculously still upright, but my brain had already decided I couldn't do it. It told me to get down low, to hug the face, and in doing so I fell flat on my own. I could have nailed it, though, if I hadn't given up – if I'd only *thought* differently.

So just try.

~

Dawn seeps through the windows, a faint glow stirring us from sleep. Liam is closest.

'How does it look?' I ask.

He fiddles to put his glasses on, squinting upwards through the smudged glass. 'Yeah, it's clear up there.'

'Right.' The nervous butterflies are back.

We climb and climb, above the tree line into the harsh, high land of rock. I skirt crags on narrow ledges crusted with white and black lichen and the silence of the still air almost rings in my ears. The scree descents seem endless, scarily steep and scattered with big chunks of rock. It's a marathon of concentration, of studying the ground, searching for the best place to put feet and poles. I focus only on where I am going, not daring to consider how far I might fall if I misjudge things. There is simply no room for any ounce of expectation that I might get it wrong. I must think like an achiever.

The sole of my boot catches on rock and I fumble. 'Come on, focus, Laura!'

We slip into a saddle then climb again, the route a vast jumble of rocks, shifting and tilting under my weight. When we finally reach it, Mount Rintoul's summit is blessedly large: proper flat ground where I don't have to worry about where my feet are. It feels fantastic.

'Check the views!' The scale is enormous, a vast grey moonscape with only the odd patch of white alpine daisies to soften it. 'Where does the trail go from here?' I scan the ridge line ahead, following it as it bends in a giant sweeping curve. There seems nothing beyond it that resembles a path.

'Ah, I think it goes around there.' Liam points a hiking pole in the direction of a long, jagged knife-edge of rock rising dramatically from our ridge. 'Just below the rocky bit.'

I squint to study the distant terrain and spy the vaguest line scraped into the dirt on what appears to be a near vertical wall of scree.

'You're *fucking* joking!' It doesn't look doable.

No one else says a word. If they're worried they're not showing it. I feel the old feelings return, of wondering how everyone else seems to know what they're doing. How did I miss out on the life training that prepared them for moments like this?

I want to stamp my feet and refuse to take part but I have no choice. The mountains aren't interested in my tantrums. I'm in the middle of the Richmond Ranges and the only way out is onward. *One step at a time, Laura, let's just tackle it when we get there.*

Orange markers guide us around the curve of the ridge then sweep us downward and I use my hiking poles to brace each tentative step. I reach a boot-wide trail – the thin scrape in the scree I saw from afar – and it's not as bad as it first seemed. It's still ridiculously steep and precarious, but doable.

I work my way over and around rocky outcrops, crouching for balance, abs aching. With thighs of jelly, I teeter on rocks, searching for foot placements. The track steepens, and grit scatters the hard surface like ball bearings. I aim for small boulders, a solid base on which to land, but even they prove untrustworthy. I stand on one half the size of my backpack and the whole thing begins a steady slide, with me on it. I edge down sideways, left foot first for a few steps then swapping to right. I step and wince down 500 metres of elevation in about two kilometres – a one in four descent – and after five punishing hours we reach Rintoul Hut, just 4.5 kilometres from where we started.

I drop to the ground and wrap my hands around my screaming knees, desperate to soothe them. They feel hot, the ache sharp. I try to breathe through the pain.

'Hey, hey! We made it over the hard bit!' Liam is jovial but I am crushed. Tired from the exertion, from the concentration, from a creeping cold I am fighting.

While the others eat lunch I unhook the blue foam roller that I've carried for 1800 kilometres and drop it to the grass. Back and forth I roll, massaging thighs with ligaments tighter than trapeze wires, so tight that the skin covering them almost feels numb. Gradually they loosen just enough to carry on, across more unforgiving land. My throat is scratchy and sore, my body flushed with heat. I fantasise about a soft bed, a big bowl of fruit salad and a snuggly soft puppy but then quickly push the thoughts aside. If I don't keep control of my mind I'll never make it.

After another five hours our hut for the night appears. I allow myself to re-engage with my senses and the tiredness is overwhelming.

'High five!' Liam holds a palm up in the air.

'I feel like shit.' I raise a hand weakly to meet his. 'Think I've got a cold brewing.'

'Really? Ah, but that won't stop *you*, will it?' he says with a confident smile before turning to unpack.

Will it stop me? I lay my beaten body on a mattress, the vinyl sucking heat from me. We are only halfway through the Richmond Ranges. I will *have* to keep going. But I am tired, so tired. I need some time, some space from the schedule. The journey I had envisioned as a meditation – hugging trees, lying in the grass, gazing at the sky, creatively framing photos, pondering life – has not come to pass. More often than not it's been a whirlwind of power walking, chores and logistics. I need to give myself time to think, to find space and answers, if I want to create the meditative and super-functioning state of inner peace I was looking for. My mind is much better than it was but still it whizzes into overdrive much of the time, replaying past scenarios and imagining future ones.

I decide I need to try to stay present. If I can't get a grip on my mind here I will have no hope when I return home. And I can't go back to how things were.

~

There's a river crossing on a rock chute just above a 4-metre waterfall … the water is flowing fast down the chute and if you lose footing, you go over the waterfall.

The morning is cold. I pull on a down jacket and wander barely 100 metres from the hut to find a hidden tarn. All is quiet and still, the tarn's surface a mirror reflecting the dark forest crowding the water's edge. The pale trunks of dead trees poke like ghostly fingers from the watery depths. A thin blanket of mist hovers above the lake, heavy and silent in the windless air.

This is what I'm here for, these moments of stillness and silent beauty. Where all I can hear is the call of a bird echoing around the tarn, its voice so clear, the air so lacking in white noise, I can hear every nuance of every note. These moments rejuvenate and realign me. Nature has always done that. When everything turns to shit, nature has a way of making things okay again.

Years ago I flapped wildly in a job I didn't know how to do with people who didn't have time to teach me. It was a seasonal gig in a ski resort, a mad rush for three months before fading to silence again over summer. I literally ran between posts, surrounded by machines spitting out reams of tickets, phones running off the hook and hundreds of punters anxious to hit the slopes. But at day's end all my troubles melted away when I left the office and huffed through the thin air towards the mountain's summit to watch the sunset. I breathed deeply at the cold, taking in views of rippling ranges against a skyline of dark blue and orange, while the land sucked the tension from my body, replacing it with a hit of endorphins. I felt as though a wise old grandmother had just put everything into perspective for me. *This is what's real. This is all that matters.* Nature's simplicity is my spirit level and her beauty my reward.

The day's agenda strikes fear into my heart again. *I might get washed over a fucking waterfall?* Seriously, should trail notes ever read like this?

The track above the Wairoa River is hardly wide enough for one boot in places, cut into the side of a valley with a sheer drop to the churning water far below. The trail notes call it sidling. I call it suicidling. We follow it for hours, in slow, deliberate steps from ledge to mossy ledge. It's off camber, rising and falling in short bursts with slippery patches of rock that shun the metal tips of my hiking poles. Hairline fractures threaten ledges of dirt and it seems just a matter of time before the whole thing gives way.

We cross the river time and again, wading through water so gin-clear it's almost tinged with blue. One more rocky cascade appears before us, draining down and out of sight over a tumble of boulders to our left. 'Is this it, do you reckon?' I frown doubtfully. The water looks about knee deep, frothing white and bouncing around the rocks, but no worse than anything we've already done. Could this be the dreaded 'river crossing on a rock chute above a waterfall'?

'Well, according to the map we're not all that far from the hut.' Liam studies his notes. 'So I think this must be it. Either that or we've already passed it.'

The water is cold but not overly strong and in seconds I am through, another feared obstacle behind me.

~

Grey alpine peaks turn to orange-brown rock and scrubby grass that reminds me of the Outback at home. We cross rivers, rock-hop boulder fields, and traverse great scree slopes while the hot sun flays us mercilessly. Sweat dribbles down my forehead, gathering on my eyelashes and dripping off the end of my nose. I wipe a finger across my forehead and flick away the droplets that sting my eyes. My own smell is starting to get to me, an essence of sweat trapped in thick hair.

Liam drops his pack next to a river slowed by rock pools. 'I'm stopping here.' He flops in the water in seconds and I follow him to sit fully clothed in a small pool cradled by boulders. It's cold but for once I embrace it, desperate to cool my overheated blood. When the chill starts to hurt I lie on a heat-warmed rock in the middle of the river with only my hair draped over the edge, the water pulling it downstream, rinsing and massaging my scalp.

Days of pain and exertion are washed away. The blue sky seems endless, mesmerising. Lying in the river's midst, the rushing water is the only sound and I feel almost swallowed up by it, merging with it. Where do I finish and the river begin? It doesn't matter. We are one. Time seems to have stopped, everything else falling away. There is no past, no future, only a now woven deeply with the rock, the air, the water. I lie there, suspended.

It's Isabel who eventually breaks the spell. 'I guess we better keep going?'

'Yeah. I guess.'

The ranges live up to their reputation – harsh, dangerous, vicious and unforgiving. Time after time we descend to huge boulder-filled riverbeds only to climb steeply back up the other side before descending again. It's so steep I fear I will slide on the loose surface back into the ravine from where I just crawled. After each river crossing I hope that the trail might ease up, that the worst might be behind us, but instead I curse out loud at the injustice of yet another stupidly sharp ascent.

'*Faaaaark!*' My lungs heave with effort.

The route is so eroded in places it can only be called a trail in the loosest sense. 'Seriously, what do you call this?' I mutter to no one in particular as I clamber up an unstable, chest-high barrier, hauling on rocks and tree roots for help. There is no one within earshot to hear my complaints anyway.

Somehow I need to skirt past a huge rock but I can't work out the best way. Should I edge beneath it on the loose scree or climb over the rock, which will have more grip but will mean I'm higher up and even more exposed? My day is full of internal groaning – resistance at *what is*. But the mountains aren't interested in my complaints or fears. They just *are*. How I make my way over them is my problem – or not.

Every molecule of energy is wrung from me, every ounce of focus. My knees are beyond sore. If this is what the South Island will be like I can't imagine how I might survive it.

Finally, the Richmond Ranges spit us out onto a slick of smooth black tarmac leading to the township of Saint Arnaud, and suddenly we're cruising – power walking towards wine and pizza.

'You have a salt stain on the back of your pants,' Isabel yells out from behind. 'It looks like an ink-blot pattern! You know, like psychologists use?'

'What does it make you think of?' I yell back.

'It makes me think you need a wash.'

9

Pleasure and Pain

A friend lives near the trailhead. For two days Isabel and I luxuriate at his house while Liam lingers in Saint Arnaud.

I haven't seen Rick in ten years. We used to work together for the same dive operator – me in the office, him on the boats. He was fit, cheeky, energetic. We kissed once or twice. He seems different now. I congratulate him on setting up his own business but, though he's jovial, I see the frown lines etched in his forehead, the tension in the eyes. Stress has left its mark on him too and, though we have fun, it's not the same.

I soap every inch of my body, shampoo my hair three times until the lather remains, loofah my sweat-pimpled buttocks and slather moisturiser over my neglected skin. I sink into a double bed with soft sheets and bask in the pleasure of abundant food and nothing to do. Three-course breakfasts seem to keep me busy right through to lunchtime.

The rest is needed. I'm lethargic, my knees still twinging in pain even negotiating the two steps to the front door of the house.

I spend a lot of time stretching and hoping that the tiredness and pain will pass.

We made it safely through the Richmond Ranges but it's impossible to ignore our good fortune with the weather. Conditions were perfect. How would rain have changed the slippery rocks, or wind the precipitous ridges, or fog the ability to see where the hell the route went when there was no ground trail to follow? Mother Nature allowed us safe passage this time but there are more challenges immediately ahead. Nelson Lakes National Park is alpine too. 'Snowstorms can strike at any time,' the guidebook says. It's the place where Andy Wyatt fell to his death, where we must tackle the Waiau Pass, where the contour lines on the map are so close together they almost appear as a solid block.

Just do your best.

~

'I can take you half the way if you like?' A woman with wild grey-blonde hair leans from the window of a clapped-out car on the edge of the highway heading back to the trailhead. 'I'm Bernadette! Sorry, the car is a bit of a mess.' Her voice is warm and gravelly.

'Oh, no problem, thanks for stopping.' Isabel takes the front seat while I open the back door where a huge black-and-white bull terrier slowly paces on a hair-covered blanket.

'Move over, Daisy!' she yells, but Daisy isn't listening. I edge my way into the seat while the dog crawls her 30-kilo frame in circles over my lap. I try to guide her to the other side and eventually we settle on just her two front paws and head in my lap.

'So where are you off to this morning?' I ask. She seems to have far too much energy and enthusiasm for seven in the morning.

'Oh, I've just finished work. Nightshift. I look after a bunch of lunatics!' She grins over her shoulder at me.

'Oh, like that, is it?' I sympathise, imagining a workplace with challenging team dynamics.

'Yeah, I'm a carer. There's an asylum down the road back there.' She nods a head in the direction we've just come.

'Oh! Right.'

She chats about work. It sounds challenging.

'How do you cope?' I ask.

'Smoke a *lot* of marijuana!' Bernadette glances at me, eyes glinting, and suddenly her smile seems a touch maniacal.

She delivers us safely to a junction and when the car has left, Isabel silently raises her eyebrows at me.

'Okay, well, *you* choose the next one, then.'

She flags down an enormous truck that rumbles to a halt in the roadside bay. I gaze up at the vertical steps leading to the cab, for the first time realising just how high they are off the ground.

Isabel goes first and then it's my turn. I grab on to the handrails, slowly yanking myself up the three steps, wrestling with a bag laden with seven days of food. I plonk down in the seat then manoeuvre my pack alongside, but the load yanks my right shoulder from its socket.

'Shit!' I drop the pack to grab the wrist of my limp arm, struck with panic. 'No, no, no!'

Isabel looks at me blankly. 'What is it?'

'I've dislocated my shoulder! I need to get down!'

Time is short. I need to bend over, to dangle my arm and hopefully let gravity pull it back into place. It needs to be done quickly, before swelling makes the job virtually impossible, but I can't do it seated in a confined space. I look at the stairs, wondering how I'm going to descend with only one functioning arm, an arm already needed to support the aching, limp one.

'Are you all right?' The driver unclips his seatbelt, running around to assist. 'I have the same problem myself sometimes.'

Fumbling, I lower myself to the road and quickly bend over, letting my arm hang. I wiggle my upper body forwards, sideways, trying to find the position where it will feel right again, where my shoulder will fall back into place. But it's not working. It doesn't feel like it usually does. It must have come out in a different direction. *Shit!*

I give my wrist a gentle tug with the other hand and at last the awful pulling sensation stops. I stand up in relief and look into the concerned face of the driver.

'Sorted,' I say softly. 'Thanks.'

One-handed, I jerk my way back up the steps to the cab and, when I'm seated, shock takes over. My shoulder aches like a demon. I want to cry but instead I sit quietly, wishing I were somewhere else. I want to bundle myself up in bed again and lick my wounds, find somewhere safe and warm to heal. I know it will take days to stop hurting, weeks to feel secure. I think it's the awful sense of vulnerability that shakes me most, the realisation of how helpless I am – one arm dangling, useless until I can find a way to get it back in, *if* I can find a way. And if I can't, then no one can help – until I find a doctor.

The truck reaches our stop and I ask Isabel to manhandle my pack back down to the ground. 'Are you going to be able to do this?' she asks.

I hope so. 'Yeah. I just need to get it onto my back. It doesn't really sit on my shoulders as such, just on my collarbone. I might just need some help … getting it … on …' I wrestle it up onto my back and once it's there my shoulder doesn't feel any worse.

Through cold drizzle we skirt the shore of a large alpine lake, both of us sluggish and softened by a few days of the good life. My body whimpers in pain. We reach Lakehead Hut in three hours and decide to go no further, instead climbing into our sleeping bags to rest. Tomorrow we must climb to Upper Travers Hut, 18 kilometres away. Liam is waiting for us there.

~

A good night's sleep and a sunny sky help. We follow a river for most of the day, climbing gently away from the lake towards the mountains. Grassland turns to forest, crisscrossed with clear bubbling streams. It's beautiful. I slip deeply into my surroundings, into the sounds of nature – the call of a bird, the rush of water, the snap of a twig. I mimic them out loud without thinking and then laugh at the strangeness of it. A vast bank of water-soaked peat moss stretches alongside me and I can't resist touching it, poking a finger deep down without reaching the bottom.

I am totally absorbed by my surroundings. The concept of me as a person, an individual with a story, seems less relevant lately. Not a fragment of my old life remains, nothing to tell me who I am, what I am. No job, no clothes, no possessions or familiar relationships that might define me. Whatever makes me *me* seems to be disappearing. It's as though I'm a plant cutting that's been grafted onto a much larger tree, our fibres fusing to become one.

For seven hours we climb, rising above the forest to an overwhelming view: an arc of rocky mountains cupping pockets of snow in their upper reaches, startlingly white against a blue sky. Nearby are waterfalls, boulder fields, piles of tree trunks strewn like matchsticks from a past avalanche. And, in the distance, nestled at the far end of the valley, lies our hut. I stop walking to take it all in and my breath catches in my throat. I feel the urge to cry but for what reason? It seems ridiculous that beauty should make me weep. But it's not just a vision. I can actually *feel* it, the immense power of the land. It's as though my heart is recognising something my brain doesn't yet understand.

~

We find Liam in a window seat at Upper Travers Hut, a relative palace with huge double-glazed windows offering mountain views as good as any five-star hotel. 'Looks like we might have the place to ourselves tonight.' He smiles.

There is no mention of Steve and Brad in the hut book. They must still be behind us and if they haven't caught us here they won't catch us on this section.

I want our paths to cross again. I know so little about Steve and what I do know could be pieced together in any number of ways. Logic tells me that Wellington was a random kiss and no more, yet the daydream of finding love in such a landscape is hard to resist.

We leave early the next morning, almost immediately coming upon a sign. *Avalanche path. No stopping.*

Shortly after is another. *Are you prepared for Travers Saddle?*

Are we? The signs start to psyche me out. My strength has returned, though, and I charge up, powered on fresh air and insane views. Above the tree line we skirt the base of the monstrous Mount Travers while clouds move swiftly around us, revealing then hiding views of the jagged grey mountains rippling into the distance.

Liam picks up something small and dark from between the rocks: a pair of men's boxer shorts. I turn them over in my hands – stretch cotton, navy, a thin red line on the waistband. 'Nope. I don't recognise them.' When the words are out, it strikes me as a funny thing to say. Do I really know all the intimate layers my fellow hikers are wearing? Pretty much.

We follow snow poles through open tussock and rock, down, down. My knees complain. The river is a constant companion, a line of white and pale blue tumbling over boulders, collecting water from all corners of the valley, from rivers, streams and waterfalls. The water cascades down sheer rock in long thin drops and bursts forth from forested flanks like a fireman's hose. The land is alive.

~

*The track climbs a steep scree slope in a direct fashion
to a high terrace. From here it is a 500-metre sidle and
climb up to Waiau Pass. Good fitness and reasonable
agility are a prerequisite for all.*

The Waiau Pass looms – the section where the contour lines are far compressed, the section that is not quite mountaineering, where Andy Wyatt died. I have worried about this place ever since I learned of its existence, since I printed the map in my office and read the description in my guidebook on the train home. My brain has fixated on it for almost a year, worrying about the unknown because that is what it has always done.

Even at the age of five I was doing it. I sat in a café booth with my mother and sister, telling them that I didn't want to start school. 'I don't know how to read!' I whimpered. 'But that's why you *go* to school,' they chimed soothingly. I remember picking up my first proper book from the library in the corner of the classroom. It had pictures of leaves changing colours with the seasons and five words per side in large type. Grimly I flicked through the pages, certain I would never master it.

New challenges have always carried a disproportionate amount of anxiety for me. You're exposed to risk, to judgement. *If you don't try you can't fail.* I never consciously repeated this mantra to myself but in retrospect it was there all the same. Of course, if I get the Waiau Pass wrong then it really will be a problem.

Almost immediately the climbing begins, up huge scree slopes and around the bluff overlooking the glacial dam of Lake Constance, where Andy fell just a month ago. I walk in his footsteps and wonder what went wrong but the fact is there are plenty of places to fall. The only real 'trail' is one that we choose ourselves, a vague, unmarked passage between two poles. Today it's sunny and still, but in bad visibility, strong winds or rain, the route would be a different beast. We descend to the lake's narrow shoreline and hike beyond it to a vast valley floor scattered with small white gentian flowers quivering on the breeze.

Ahead the valley finishes but I can see no trail. Our way is blocked by a semi-circle of mountains, disturbingly steep. There is nowhere for us to go but up. The little voice inside starts to protest. It's not a voice that really knows what it's talking about just yet; it doesn't have all the facts. I realise it's my autopilot, just a programmed response to fear and challenge. No one is interested in hearing it, not my companions, or the mountains or the trail. I stifle the urge to voice it and keep walking, scanning, searching, studying the mountains ahead. I spy a thin grey line scoured into the gravel on what appears to be a fairly sheer face. It must be our track. *Fuck, seriously.*

I'm sick of these moments. There have been so many I've lost count. I've feared the terrain, feared the journey, worried whether or not I was up to it. But so far I've always made it through. There has been more fear in the imagining of things than in the reality of them, and worry is just a waste of precious energy. Better to take things one step at a time, assess them as they come.

I pace slowly, climbing shards of loose rock that clink and shift under my boots. The slippery gravel becomes almost too steep to climb. If I lean too far forward my feet will slide out from under me, too far back and I'll end up doing a backward roll. Either way would be bad. There'd be no stopping until the bottom, hundreds of metres below.

Like a mountaineer I stamp the toes of my boots into the face several times for a secure grip. I dig my poles in, testing them for anchor before hoisting myself up. Each step is the same. Always I keep at least three points of contact with the ground. All matters, aside from the correct placing of bodily parts, slide into the background – the great view behind me, the climb that I'd like to film. Every drop of focus is aimed at a safe ascent.

A small grassy terrace half an hour shy of the pass provides blessed flat ground and we drop our packs for a rest, silenced by the breathtaking peaks just higher than us. Isabel and I recline against a large, warm rock, sheltered from the wind, fingers laced behind heads, faces turned to the sun. I feel as though I'm relaxing in a deckchair in the upper regions of some European ski resort.

'I suppose we should get up that pass, no?' Liam interrupts quietly.

When we at last crest it, the sudden skyline of jagged grey is immense. White snow lies cradled in dips and hollows. Everywhere is rock – beneath me, around me – huge slips of it, small chunks of it. I can almost see how the landscape formed – mountains pushing upwards while grass and rocks and anything else that couldn't cope with the sheer angle slid further down.

The clack of poles echoes around the mountains. '*Cooo-eeee!*' I holler at them. They holler faintly back. 'You have a go, Isabel.'

'Whooooo!'

We laugh, enjoying the freedom of yelling at the tops of our voices without consequence.

'Your turn, Liam. Go on, no one can hear you out here.'

His voice falters. '*Aaaarrrr, aaarrrr!*' It's the kind of sound you make when you want to make a loud sound but you don't want anyone to hear you.

The descent is gentle at first but suddenly the poles disappear from sight and we fan out in search of orange.

'There's one here.' Liam nods downwards.

I walk over and follow his gaze. 'Gosh.' It's steep, very steep. Just a mass of craggy rock with sections of sheer slabs veined with cracks.

Isabel makes a start on a particularly blocky section but pauses moments into it. 'Oh, shit!'

'Are you all right?' I call out.

'Argh … shit … shit.' She faces the rock, arms clinging outstretched above, feet searching for a foothold. 'Oh … I got it.' She lowers herself, muttering unhappily.

I crouch down, searching for a good place to begin, opting for a backside slide. I stretch my legs out to slip section by section, catching my heels on tiny nobs and crevices. The steepest bit is probably 50 metres long and, with the worst of it over, I turn to watch Liam. He descends a crevice between two slabs, face to face with its grey hardness, and even with his long limbs he looks small against it.

The steepness continues but now I can use my poles to help balance, teetering on tiny outcrops and ignoring the precipitous gully just a boot-length away. I think I've been hardened to it now, all this scrambling and exposure. There's been so much of it lately I'm starting to think about it less and less. Like a wildebeest crossing a crocodile-infested river, I follow the others on our southern migration, forging on despite the dangers because there is simply no other way.

The grey rock peters out to meet a grassy terrace. In the middle, a small blue waterhole shimmers. We soak our feet in its icy water and eat lunch under the gaze of the mountains, and I feel unbelievably lucky to be here. The air is so crisp and clean I want to drink it deep into my lungs. The crossing is behind us and the relief seems to have unleashed a boundless appreciation for the beauty around us. Bit by bit, nature is cracking me open, releasing me like a nut from its shell. Each challenge requires a surrender to *what is* and each success delivers a greater awareness, openness and confidence.

I lean in close for a photo with Liam and suddenly, unexpectedly, a buzz of electricity shoots through me. I don't know what to make of it.

Did he feel it too?

Like a light switch flicked, I suddenly *see* him – khaki shirt flapping open to reveal a broad chest lightly flecked with hair, the tanned hands unwrapping a chocolate bar to raise it to his full lips. I see the short stubble beneath his nose and across his cheeks, the eyes hidden behind thin, gold-rimmed aviator sunglasses. His brown hair is damp with sweat, slicked this way and that. *Damn*, he looks like a movie star! How did I not notice it?

I've never paid so much attention to him, never studied his features, but the unexpected touch of skin has triggered something. His quiet nature allowed him to blend into the background, and I never bothered to investigate. Liam was just Liam. Quiet, shy, a little awkward.

Well …

~

The pale blue water of the Waiau River cascades over the occasional waterfall, idling in clear pools before bouncing on. A sheltered camp spot appears amongst the beech trees. It's pretty but Isabel wants to keep going. An hour later she slips, landing heavily on a tree stump that stabs her in the ribs. She lies there for a minute, gasping in pain.

'My feet are tired. They're tripping.'

We sit quietly until she is ready to move on, sharing the weight of her pack to ease her load.

Caroline Creek Bivvy is no bigger or more salubrious than a garden shed so we pitch tents instead. Liam lights a fire in a stone pit. I watch him out of the corner of my eye and he smiles back shyly. Is that his usual smile or is it something else? It *feels* different, but maybe it's all in my head.

The pitter-pattering on the flysheet sounds like rain but is hordes of sandflies; beyond them is the sound of a river that never sleeps. I lie in my tent, enlivened by the energy around me.

~

In the morning I step out of my tent and reach an arm back to pull on my jacket and the sound of gristle and bone grinding accompanies a sudden, godawful pain.

'No!'

My shoulder. I bend over in a panic, frantically trying to wiggle it back into place. I lean forward, then backward. I dangle my arm, give it a gentle tug. It's a bad one, much worse than before.

No, no, no! Please don't let this happen out here!

With a clunk it finally drops into place and I collapse onto a log, doubled over and clutching my arm. The joint screams and moans, stretched too many times.

I follow the usual gamut of emotion – pain, shock, then tears followed by the terrible feeling of vulnerability and the realisation that this happens too often, too easily. And what would happen if I couldn't get it back in place? How would I get help out here? It would take many painful hours before any help could respond to the satellite alert of my personal locator beacon. What if I'd done it yesterday, climbing down the Waiau Pass? What if, what if …?

I cry quietly into the neck of my fleece, anxious to pull myself together before the others surface, but the wind has been knocked out of me. I slouch on the log, trying to muster the energy to take my tent down. Sore and delicate, all I really want is a comforting hug and to lie down and rest. I don't want to do this today.

An hour later I'm doing it: 28 kilometres that take me a total of nine hours. When I reach Anne Hut I cry again. I tell Liam and Isabel about my shoulder but I hide the pain – I don't need to bother them about it.

The next day is easier. Just five hours to Boyle Flat Hut. I sleep and revive and listen to music, relishing the rarity of a free afternoon.

I avoid sudden movements with my arm. I must not reach sideways. Or back, or up. And I must not lie awkwardly. If I do any of these things I feel the bone lifting slightly in its socket. I pull the ache against my body, right elbow cradled by left hand. *Keep it close, Laura. Keep it close.*

The sandflies are vicious, swarming around the doors and windows, scratching on them like vampires. A long afternoon turns to evening. Isabel and I cook dinner early and then there is nothing to do but watch Liam prepare his. Slowly, methodically, he grabs handfuls of dry couscous, trying to carry them to his pot without dropping any. We watch as tiny grains bounce across the table. Then he slides open a ziplock bag and pours in the remainder of his dried mushrooms. We're transfixed by his every move. It's like TV for the outdoors.

He looks up, suddenly noticing his audience, and we all laugh. This is ridiculous.

~

Hanmer Springs cuts our route, a small tourist town built around hot springs and mountain sports. It's Valentine's Day and after punishing myself so thoroughly I decide to treat myself to a massage, complete with fluffy white robe and a soak in the hot springs next door. The young masseuse is reluctant to treat me though, my recent medical history making her nervous.

'Um, I really don't think it's appropriate for me to massage you so soon after you've had two dislocations.'

'I'm fine, it's no problem.'

'I mean, have you seen a doctor?'

'It's not necessary, I do this regularly, I know my body.'

'It's just that …'

'Just give me a massage!'

She does, and it's fantastic.

I soak in the hot springs and pad, barefoot, to a dressing room filled with sweet-smelling potions. In front of a full-length mirror I pull the tie from around my waist, letting the robe fall to the floor. The reflection makes me gasp.

What has happened to my body?

My head looks far too big for it, for a start. I've always had a narrow frame but without any excess fat on it I now look like a prisoner of war. The tops of my ribs are visible. I stand sideways and laugh out loud. I'm so ridiculously thin it doesn't seem possible. Perhaps this is just one of those 'skinny mirrors'?

I *feel* strong so the vision doesn't concern me but it's clear my body needs more fuel.

~

Steve and Brad walk into town the night before we leave, trailing a group of hikers I've never met – two pretty young American girls, a Frenchman, a Kiwi girl and Brad's brother. It's someone's birthday and there are drinks on the town.

I am torn, seeing Steve and Liam side by side – one with tonnes of personality, a little rougher around the edges, the other shy, yet tall and good-looking, perhaps with more facets of his personality yet to be revealed.

Liam and I seem to be talking more, sharing more, but maybe that is my doing. Whatever is going on in his head remains a mystery.

Steve throws an arm casually around my shoulders, lightly twining my hair through his fingers, stroking it faintly as we talk about nothing. My heart pounds. So much time has passed. We've barely spoken. I feel awkward, unsure of the part I should be playing.

People are everywhere; there's raucous yelling and laughing. I want to go to bed.

Steve folds his arms around me in a giant bear hug, kissing me just to the side of my lips. 'Good night, Laura.'

~

I return to the trail with Liam and Isabel, delving deeper into the Canterbury wilderness, relishing its rawness. We are back in the land of rushing rivers, birds, wind in trees: back in the land of simple living.

Days pass, kilometres pass. We've done just over two thousand of them now. A natural hot spring bubbles into a perfect spa-sized pool nestled against a rocky escarpment. It is divine except for the hordes of sandflies that flit up my nose and snag in my lashes. The day ends up being a short one. It seems it's impossible to do a serious work-out after a hot bath.

I try to dissect my time with Steve in Hanmer. It was an odd reunion, just a few hours long and crowded with other people. He was touchy-feely yet the 'good night' made no sense. I'd sent him a message. *Do you think we'll ever kiss again?*

It'd be nice, hey, he responded. *Maybe later. In Bluff.*

Bluff, the very end of our journey.

Then later, another message. *Things are different on the trail.*

They sure are.

~

The rivers are everywhere, winding through the valleys littered with tree trunks dumped by floods. Some are big enough to make our hiking poles quiver in the current, while others are simply banks of pebbles lying in wait for the river to expand. For hours we walk over them, pebbles too small to rock hop but big enough to pitch a boot sideways. They shift and roll with each step, sucking energy from us. None of us are great fans of the riverbed.

Trail markers are scarce, our guide, instead, the natural features. The trail notes tell us to follow valleys, crossing and re-crossing the river 'as necessary'. We take care choosing where to cross but ultimately rivers no longer concern us. We plough through them, one after another.

I lift my gaze one afternoon from the pebbles to the vast valley around – dark trees, the mighty river, banks of low cloud. I recognise the scene. It could be straight out of my guidebook back home – a picture of complete wilderness that once rattled the butterflies in my stomach. It had looked so riddled with danger back then. Now it just feels like home.

I realise I'm not thinking about Frank much anymore and if I do it's with a kind of distant interest. I think I was there just to complete his image, a man with every box that success demanded be ticked, including the relationship. I don't think he really knew what it meant to be close to someone, to be honest, to be real. Neither of us knew what love was. He didn't know how to give it and I didn't know what it should feel like. It all seems pretty sad now. Anyway, he's not my problem anymore. I have no energy for anger, no appetite for it.

The trail is faint but our eyes are experienced, three pairs better than one for searching out the sporadic orange markers. Our team is harmonious. We walk at similar speeds and we like to keep the same schedule but there is no pressure to hike together. We go at our own pace, starting the day when we choose, having breaks as we choose. Sometimes we walk alone, meeting up for lunch or a snack break, and always we meet at day's end. We are free yet supported. It works for all of us.

Other hikers are few and far between. We may walk a week without seeing anyone and even then the encounters are brief.

Isabel is my mentor, my sounding-board. We talk about writing, about boys. She listens to me prattle on about Steve and Liam, the hypothetical question of who would be better for me if I had the choice. 'Just kiss them both!' She laughs, exasperated.

I feel a warmth blooming, for others, for *everyone*. I have time, patience. I am untroubled, gloriously happy. I start to sing. A lot.

When I'm alone I hike and sing at the top of my voice. Sometimes I have to pause my walking so that I have the necessary puff to do justice to a crescendo. I don't just sing songs, I sing sentences too. 'It's *din-ner tiiiime!*' Isabel starts to call me Jingles.

We laugh often, sometimes uncontrollably.

At the end of a snack break I watch Isabel put her trail shoes back on. She pauses after lifting up one shoe, frowning at something inside before fishing it out and popping it in her mouth.

'Isabel, did you just eat a peanut from your shoe?'

We are consumed with laughter, which continues through the afternoon as more things amuse us. Later she sneezes with such force that the clips on the chest strap of her backpack burst open. At Hope Shelter, Liam kits himself out in full armour against the sandflies; the hut is so dilapidated the flies move freely between the gaps in the floorboards. Though the evening is mild he lies bundled in a sleeping bag, wearing a face net, hat and gloves to cover any exposed skin. We're hysterical with laughter. We try to stop, to focus on going to sleep, but someone stifles a giggle and then we're off again.

I've never laughed so often, so freely and with such little stimulus. Is it simply delirium brought on from tiredness, or is it that we are so light in being? I don't know. I don't care. Life is good. Life is *great*.

~

Progress through the South Island is scarily fast. Unlike the meandering route of the north, it now charges directly, relentlessly, towards our finish. We can see the kilometres, and our big adventure, slipping away. Perhaps only another six weeks or so remain. None of us are happy about it.

Liam hopes to be made redundant from work on his return – a company payout would send him back to the wilds for months. Isabel is less concerned – she loves her job – though she will miss New Zealand and the trail. She begins watching the calendar closely, counting the days until her partner arrives for a week of togetherness. The pause in her schedule will mean we part ways for good.

And what of me? So much of the last year has been geared towards planning this adventure and then actually doing it. I've never thought beyond the end of the hike. That time seemed to occur in some mystical faraway place where I had achieved my dream, become strong and happy. Where I'd become a conqueror who had mastered her universe, facing only a road to future glories. Everything would be good then, I imagined. I never really thought about how that would play out. I was too busy surviving the now to think about the future.

But now the future is only six weeks away and I know what will happen. The world will go on and I will go back to the city, to my job, to everything I disliked before I left. The swivel chair and desk that tied knots in my back and neck, the mouse that made my forearm hurt, the furore of the city, its gritty air. A life restricted, existing only to live on weekends, and the possibility that anxiety might be there, waiting to greet me as I step off the plane.

It all seems impossibly awful. I feel a squeeze in my chest.

~

Sometimes Liam and I walk together, just the two of us. The atmosphere feels strange, like something is half going on but not. He seems to loiter with intent, like perhaps he wants to say something but he never does. Instead he just looks awkward and smiles.

The sun sinks on another day while the two of us stand on a bridge, leaning against its railings. Isabel has raced off ahead, keen to get closer to town to meet the date of her imminent rendezvous with her partner. With just the two of us, his body is far closer to mine than usual. I prod him gently with a finger and he yawns, a noisy, full-body yawn.

'You look like you're ready for bed,' I say. 'Shall we go back?'

'No, no, I'm good!'

It looks like something is on his mind. He stands very close, closer than ever. I turn sideways slightly and smile at him, waiting. He grins shyly but his eyes remain fixed on the distant sun, which casts a metallic sheen on the river below. I study his face, flushed in the cool evening air. Even his ears are sweating.

The sun has nearly gone.

'Let's go back,' I say.

We wander to the tents but again he seems to stall. We both stand there for a few long seconds.

'Well … goodnight, then, Liam.' I retreat inside.

'Goodnight.'

~

*Follow the Deception River through the lower gorge,
recrossing the river where necessary. Trampers can pick
their way upwards, mostly in the riverbed. There is a final
steep climb over rough terrain to get up to the Goat Pass Hut.*

The next morning Liam is quiet, even more so than usual.

'Are you all right?' I ask.

'Yeah, I'm fine.'

His long legs move swiftly over the river pebbles for hours. My legs can't keep up so I let him go. We meet again at lunchtime and he seems lost in thought, a little moody even.

'Is it my imagination or are you a little quiet today?'

'No, everything's fine.'

For an entire day I follow the Deception River towards its source high in the mountains. The river becomes steeper, narrower, and our route disappears into a maze of angular boulders. There is no grace in my technique. On all fours or even on my belly, I haul myself up the gorge by any means possible. I climb until the river is reduced to a relative trickle a few metres wide, and beyond it sits Goat Pass Hut, perched on the edge of a sheer valley. Patches of snow dot the peaks and the mountains reverberate with the screeching of keas. It's good to hear them. The world's only alpine parrot, they've become increasingly rare. Intelligence makes them inquisitive rogues, infamous for ripping the rubber off windscreen wipers and other destructive forms of play. Their numbers dropped from about 150,000 to 5000 in the mid-1800s following a campaign by farmers to cull them, and even though they're now protected, kea deaths seem to continue.

Hikers are advised to be alert to the possibility of shredded shoelaces on boots left outside, or anything else for that matter. 'It's when you *can't* hear them that you need to worry,' a ranger tells me. 'That's when they're getting up to mischief.'

Isabel hasn't progressed beyond the hut and the three of us are reunited again, sitting on the deck, taking in the views, watching the sun sink. I notice a hole in the back of Liam's shirt and finger it gently. He flinches.

'I'm going to bed. I'm tired,' he says, suddenly getting up.

'He's definitely quieter today,' Isabel murmurs once he's gone.

I don't know what is going on in his head. But then I never have.

At midnight I sneak outside for a wee and the sky is astonishing, the moon glowing like a huge spotlight on pockets of snow in the peaks. Stars glitter. I breathe deep.

~

Isabel and I leave early in the morning for the last ten kilometres to the village of Arthur's Pass. Liam sleeps in.

'We'll see you there,' I whisper before heading out. 'We'll book you a bed.'

He mumbles acknowledgement from his bunk but doesn't budge.

We keep a good pace, arriving in time for lunch – a huge chicken and vegetable curry in a cafe – and I check my emails. The office crew back home are taking bets on whether I'll be back.

My job. I am lucky to have the security of one to go back to but I cannot muster any enthusiasm for it. I envy Isabel and the career she has forged from writing. It must be incredible to do something that inspires you, something creative.

Still full from lunch, Isabel and I wander to a pub for dinner.

'So I was reading Joe's blog about the section coming up,' I say. 'We've got two or three relatively straightforward days but then south of Methven he reckons it's pretty tough. Chest-high tussock grass, no ground trail to follow, forty-five stream crossings in one day! Plus the highest alpine pass on the trail and then we've got the Rangitata in there.'

The Rangitata River: a mighty braided shape-shifter whose flow spreads across a valley about four kilometres wide. No one can be entirely sure at any particular moment whether the multitude of waterways within it are safe to cross. A hiker may successfully cross the first half of shingle and streams only to come across a braid too deep or fast to be passable, and water levels change rapidly here. The trail designers have declared it a hazard zone that poses 'a significant danger to trampers on foot'. We are urged not to risk it.

'Ah, the usual TA fun,' Isabel says with a grin. 'Apparently you can organise a road transfer around it or rent a boat or something.'

'Yeah, it looks expensive and complicated, though. I've heard of a few hikers who got through recently. The rivers have all been pretty low so far. It would be much easier if we could just walk through.'

'Totally,' she says. 'I'm not sure what I'll do yet when I reach it.'

It will be sad to say goodbye to Isabel. Her partner is just days away and when she does arrive they will feast on food and wine for a week before rejoining the trail as a couple, a few hundred kilometres behind us. In just days our perfect trio will lose a leg, leaving just me and a man of mystery.

'Well, I guess Liam and I will suss it out when we get there.'

~

I find him back at the hostel, leaning over maps with Christian – the Parisian hiker we'd met in Hanmer Springs. Small in frame and with a bushy ginger beard that looks too big for his face, he reminds me of a garden gnome.

I pour a glass of wine and sit at the far end of the table to listen in on the game plan.

'The route starts from here with two to three hours on a track right next to the highway.' Christian taps a finger on the map. 'Then it joins the Harper River Track for two to three days.'

Liam leans in closer to see, skewering a sausage on a fork from the plate between them. 'Well, it's about seven to eight hours of trail to the first hut on the Harper Pass Track so I'm going to skip that road section and get straight up to the hut for tomorrow night.'

My stomach drops like a stone. *And me?*

I look up at him, waiting for further information, an explanation, some discussion or corroboration, maybe. There is none. If I hike the roadside trail I will not catch him by tomorrow night without an epic effort. But if he doesn't care whether we stick together or not then there's no point. Why strive to maintain a team he doesn't care for?

The conversation continues but I no longer hear it. I leave my wine on the table to escape to our room, blindly shoving things in my pack while the blood rushes in my brain. Within minutes the door opens. It's Liam. He enters, leaning against the bunk in front of me with a sheepish smile, looking more awkward than ever.

'Ah, I'm sorry. I've got to do what I've got to do, no?' He speaks softly. 'I mean, I can't walk sections I don't want to, this is my holiday too, right?'

'Sure,' I say briskly. *To avoid three hours of roadside walking?*

'I mean, I've enjoyed walking with you but I don't suppose we'll see each other tomorrow night.' He's smiling, trying to lighten the situation. 'So I guess this is goodbye, then.' He takes a step forward, opening his arms for a hug.

I stare at them, speechless. *This is it? This is how it ends?* For three months we have done everything together, planned everything, but now this, without warning, without discussion, a plan I simply overheard.

Emotions fly quicker than I can make sense of, blocking all rational thought. I hug him briefly – my arms barely touching his back, my face turned away – then return to my packing.

10

Alone

Methven. The small everyday noises on the street make me flinch. Dizziness floods my brain like a king tide, swirling and blurring my vision. Chest and throat are locked tight. No air can penetrate deep enough to be of any use. I beg for it to *please, please let me go*.

I sit on a park bench with one hand on my chest, trying to calm my breathing, trying to regroup. Tomorrow I must walk south into the Clent Hills and from there over the remote Two Thumb Range. Into the chest-high tussock, the trail-less routes, the high alpine passes and dreaded Rangitata. I can't believe my friend has left me at such a point, knowing I will be on my own. It makes me sad. I must have greatly overestimated our friendship.

My worst fears have been realised – being alone at a critical point.

There is no one on the trail in my vicinity now except Steve and Brad. I try to contact them but there is no response – they must be out of range. I have no idea where they are but I can't afford to wait. Every day brings us closer to winter. Already snow is forecast for as low as 1300 metres in a few days, though I calculate I should be well below 1000 metres by then.

I do my chores on autopilot then lie on the bed in my single room, reading trail notes and maps. Thoughts spiral, intense and chaotic, but by evening I pass through the eye of the storm and the winds shift, hurt turning to anger. Up to this point I wasn't the only one keen for the security that company provided. Now I feel discarded, no longer required.

You did want to try walking on your own, a voice of reason quietly interrupts my rant.

Yeah, not here, though! I retort.

A message from Paris beeps through on my phone. Antoine wants to know whether I am still hiking with Liam. I tell him I'm alone.

Alone? No, not completely, you've got nature with you. His words soothe me. It's true. How can I be alone? Nature has always made me feel better.

Kiwi Scout drops me a line too, checking in on my progress. I tell him where I am and that I am nervous. 'The next section is challenging but you'll do fine,' he says. 'Do you have someone to check in with for safety? If not, I volunteer!'

I feel a rush of gratitude. I don't dare tell my mum or anyone else in my family that I am walking solo. Better to leave my progress status in the hands of someone who understands what I'm undertaking.

The inevitability of going forth solo starts to sink in. I feel bolstered knowing Antoine and Kiwi Scout are rooting for me. Belle, too, sends me a lengthy message saying she has every faith in me, not that she has any idea what I'm dealing with.

Some subconscious part of me understands that I need to change my attitude. *This is going to happen so let's just look forward*, it says. *Lift your head, think positive, have a go. Trust yourself.*

And besides, there's something else I've been forgetting.

I'm a fucking legend.

~

I wake refreshed and strangely eager to get going. I'm *actually* looking forward to it.

The mountains look different here, more barren and open, covered in short dry grass and pale crushed rock. I climb steadily, fully exposed to the beating sun. The air rings with a high-pitched clicking while an indefinable wave of movement ripples before me, a sea parting as I walk. My vision locks on one of the culprits, a tiny grasshopper. One gets caught in the plaits of my hair, clicking furiously, and my ears ring for half a minute or so.

The terrain has changed but I feel a shift in my mental landscape too. I stop to rest under the weight of eight days of food but it doesn't matter anymore. No one is waiting for me. I can stop and take photos, take as much time as I want. I'm a free agent. Surely I have accumulated enough skills now to find my way along 'lightly marked' trails and across rivers and such. Only the element of the unknown has the potential to pose a challenge, but even this just gives me a vague tingle of excitement. The week ahead will hold a good mix of tests. Bring it.

Comyns Hut rests in the cradle of a sweeping valley. In the river next to it I wash the salt and dust from my body and clothes and they dry quickly in the hot wind. I drag a chair to the doorway of the hut and survey the mountains around me. *So far so good. One day alone and all is well.* I give myself a little pat on the back. Actually, I quite like it – being out here on my own. All this space, all mine.

For at least half an hour I savour it.

Then Christian turns up, the gnome from Paris.

Then Thomas from Germany.

Then Johannes from Germany and Eric from the USA.

Oh.

I've never come across so many new TA hikers in one hut. It's slightly disappointing.

Everyone pores over maps and notes, working out ambitious onward plans, but I'm glad not to have to consult with anyone else. I will simply listen to my body, let *it* call the shots.

Cloud pulls over the valley, cooling the air. Outside, the wind whistles noisily. Tiny puffs slip through gaps in the old iron walls, tickling my face. In the bunk above, Johannes munches away on something particularly crunchy.

'What's that you're eating, Johannes?'

'Mmm … gingernut biscuits.'

'Ah, I've seen a lot of gingernuts on this trip.' I say, recalling how often the iconic New Zealand biscuit has appeared in someone's pack. Only when the words are out of my mouth does a double entendre rise to mind and I stifle a fit of the giggles. No one else seems to notice. Where is Isabel when I need her?

~

Trampers are required to pick their own route between markers which, in poor weather, may not be visible from one to the next. The physical and navigational challenges rise accordingly.

Johannes, Eric and Thomas are gone before I'm properly awake.

I pack up and leave Christian behind to head off alone, following a well-worn path to a river that I will follow for hours. Only once I've crossed it do I realise that I've gone the wrong way. I curse my stupidity. A few hundred metres ahead, the river bends back on itself, revealing in the riverbed far below an orange pole. Rather than backtrack I search for a more direct route. Open terrain hints at an easy escape but thickets of stiff and prickly gorse appear to block my way. I try other routes, rising and descending different lines like a mouse in a maze, but each path ends with either a steep cliff or a line of impenetrable bushes. Whenever I get within metres of a clear path, another barrier suddenly appears. I try to force a way through a line of gorse but it's impossible. Thinking I could push my way through a few metres of it is like thinking I could push my way through a few metres of coiled barbed wire.

Fuck.

Tears of frustration prickle my eyes but I'm too annoyed with myself to let them flow. What an idiot!

I finally stumble on a clear route, reaching my beloved poles forty-five minutes after leaving the hut. What a waste of energy. I should have backtracked and started again. Now Christian is bound to be way ahead of me, no doubt wondering where I am. How will I explain this one?

I study the notes carefully now. 'Travel quickly becomes confined to the stream bed and involves frequent river crossings.' I follow it for more than five kilometres, winding back and forth dozens of times, then up a saddle to traverse enormous banks of scree and swathes of tussock, chest high in places. Narrow rivulets stay hidden until I lose a boot in them. Random holes appear, the size of a large dinner plate and seeming to go nowhere but Middle-earth. I move tentatively, prodding the ground ahead with my poles. Long, golden spears of Spaniard grass grow stiff and sharp as the point of a blade, piercing me with a ferocity that makes me yelp and draws blood.

On a ridge top I down my pack to eat lunch. The morning's been tough but I'm doing it. I crossed the rivers, I braved the tussock and so far I haven't lost myself – well, not for long anyway. Daniel Boone once wrote, 'I can't say as ever I was lost, but I was bewildered once for three days.' I count myself also as temporarily bewildered. And I feel quite chuffed.

Big banks of cloud gather on the horizon. The air has chilled considerably since yesterday though no doubt the altitude makes a difference.

Five hours later, on the flatlands of the Heron Basin, I am tired but swept along by Basement Jaxx. I sing out loud to their songs, bopping away in my head, so pumped that I miss the turn-off to Double Hut. Only when I'm a full kilometre past the junction do I realise my mistake.

How did I manage that? Idiot. Another failure.

I study the notes. Backtrack two kilometres to Double Hut or advance another four to Manuka? The ground is flat now, a vague four-wheel drive track drifting in and out over the valley floor. There's probably only half an hour difference in it. I push on.

The wind suddenly turns icy, as though a freezer door has opened, and I stop to pull a raincoat over my t-shirt. Dark clouds funnel through the valley ahead, charging towards me, growing in size and deepening to a gunmetal grey. I pick up the pace.

Only about three more kilometres. Maybe just over half an hour? I console myself with the thought of the dry hut waiting. So I'll cop a little rain. How bad can things get?

The rain arrives, peppered with little balls of ice. I walk quicker, skipping over the uneven ground, pausing to search out the distant poles while wind and hail make my hands red raw. I haven't asked Mum to post my gloves over yet; it's only the last day of summer. I hold my hands behind my back to shield them, then try to shove them in my pockets but they are so numb I can't be sure I've succeeded unless I look.

In disbelief I watch the hail turn to snow. Panic floods my gut as some primal part of me recognises the seriousness of the situation. Ice in the wind, ice in my face. How far to the hut? I need to get there. The notes say it's 'hidden' up a side stream. I turn my back to the wind, stabbing clumsily at the buttons of my GPS, my fingers now useless stumps. Are they pressing the buttons or just touching them? Only when the screen responds can I tell.

I feel my core temperature dropping like a stone. I hurry on, stumbling and tripping over small rocks embedded in the dirt. 'Come on, Laura.' I speak sternly, trying to ignore the rising fear.

I start singing to sharpen my mind, keep it focused. 'Ten green bottles, hanging on the wall …' My singing is no longer joyous. This singing has purpose. 'And if one green bottle should accidentally fall, there'll be nine green bottles …' If I can't count the bottles backwards I'll know I'm in trouble.

The air is white.

I spot the turn-off to the hut: '500 metres/10 mins'.

Ten minutes is too long! The icy wind slashes at my body, beating me over and over with blows of pain to my feet, my face, my hands, my thighs. I can feel the situation slipping.

'Come on, Laura! Focus.' I raise my voice, trying to gain the attention of a mind starting to waiver. I'm out of my depth, unsure what to do, but there's only one thing I can do. 'Come on!' The voice urges me onwards.

An old corrugated iron hut comes into view. It's not far away and yet I don't feel its security. I still need to reach it; weirdly, I'm not absolutely certain I can.

Maybe 100 metres to go? There are two small streams to cross. I plunge in, wading through water that feels warm on my feet.

Twenty metres to go.

The hut door opens. Christian is holding it for me. I charge past him.

Safe.

'What happened to you?' he asks.

'The weather turned!' My voice is cheery, belying the fear I felt minutes earlier, playing down the near disaster. My frozen fingers scrape clumsily over the ice-encrusted clips on the front of my pack. Christian sees me fumbling and helps undo them.

'I was worried,' he says.

'Yeah, I took a wrong turn at the start there so I ended up

behind you. Sorry.' I hold my hands out and he wraps his around them to warm them up.

'I'm glad you got here. I was going to wait another fifteen minutes and if you weren't here by then I was going to go back to Double Hut and look for you.' He looks out the window, to the swirling snow, and then gives me a relieved smile. 'I wasn't looking forward to going out there again though.'

~

It's a cold night. Christian lends me his jacket to lay over my sleeping bag. In the morning I walk to the stream, plunging a water bottle beneath the surface. It feels painfully icy against my hands, the same water that had felt warm on my feet the night before. It could so easily have gone horribly wrong. I gaze up at a landscape transformed, sun shining brilliantly on virgin white peaks, the air still – truly the calm after the storm.

We're only at 800 metres; snow wasn't part of the plan. Two days ago I was sweltering in heat and yet yesterday – yesterday was so different. I'd read about the weather here, heard this could happen, but experiencing it is sobering.

I leave the hut on my own and come across some hunters. I ask them about the Rangitata. They think I should be fine to do it. 'Just make sure the water isn't cloudy, and don't go anywhere near it if a nor'-wester is blowing!'

One is forecast for tomorrow night.

Christian catches me and together we hike 33 kilometres of grass plains, a golden carpet between the snowy mountains.

From a high plateau in the late afternoon we see it, a mighty river shining like a long silver plait far below – the Rangitata.

In the early morning we reach its fringes, a river valley nearly five kilometres across from where we stand. It's pebble city. Ribbons of water appear as flat lines on the horizon, revealing no clues on depth or width. It's impossible to see where our best route across might be. We tackle it one braid at a time, avoiding pockets that flow swift and deep. The river is so vast big black cows graze on the small bushes in its midst. It takes hours but finally the braids dwindle away, leaving nothing but dry stones. The Rangitata is behind us.

Eight more kilometres of pebbles lead us up the length of Bush Stream with at least fifteen more river crossings. Ankles roll, boots slide, feet go nowhere. Endless freaking pebbles.

Crooked Spur Hut sits just above the tree line, another patchwork of rusted corrugated iron and concrete, basic but cosy with an eclectic mix of decor additions: an old tin cabinet containing a jar of Vegemite well past its use-by date, a pair of white towelling hotel slippers and an orange clothbound book entitled *French Tales of Our Time*. I try to coerce Christian into reading me some but he won't.

It rains a lot overnight. In the morning I walk outside to find a light dusting of snow on the peaks of the Two Thumb Range, where we are headed. Unsettled clouds hurry overhead in the wind. I go back inside to report back to Christian.

'It's been snowing.'

'Only a little bit over there.' Christian points at the range behind us.

'No, I reckon it's been snowing all around, but the sun just hasn't melted it on that face yet. It doesn't look great to me.'

'It'll be fine.'

I go through the motions of getting ready but only half-heartedly. Christian is packed, almost ready to go while my gear still lies strewn all over my bunk.

I go outside again and stare up at the mountains.

'Are you coming?' Christian calls.

I pull out my compass, noting the wind is blowing from the north-west. *Continue on with Christian or stay here until it looks better?*

'Um … I don't think so.'

'Come on, stop worrying!'

It's my call to make.

I can't help but think of the many times I have done what others said against my own judgement. The countless pairs of jeans I've bought a size too small on the urging of a shop assistant though they felt uncomfortable. 'They stretch a lot. You need to go smaller, trust me,' they said. I would never wear them more than once. The boyfriend who insisted I put his flowers in a beautiful etched earthen pot I'd lugged all the way home from Nicaragua. 'I don't think it's meant to hold water,' I said doubtfully, thinking of its porous interior. 'What's the point of a pot if you can't put water in it!' he said, and in the flowers went. They did look lovely in it – for a day. After that the water soaked through to its exterior, spoiling the beautiful paintwork forever.

If I'd listened to my gut I never would have stayed with Frank. I'd have left at those first early signs, which warned me of danger just as surely as the skies are now.

I look over at the mountains we have to cross. What is beyond them? How is the weather there? It's impossible to know until we climb up and have a look. 'It's just that we're heading towards the highest point on the whole trail. Who knows what's going on over that range, and we'll be kind of committed once we leave here. I don't think conditions look good for that.' I say, thinking out loud.

'Well, I'm going,' he says. 'Are you *sure* you don't want to come?'

I look at the clouds boiling over the mountain tops. There's something about them, something I recognise. The clouds are white-grey with an odd texture; they look thick with something. They look like the ones that funnelled up the valley towards me two days ago.

'No. I'm not going.'

He shakes his head. 'All right, then …'

I watch him make his final preparations and feel a rush of relief bound with a sense of absolute freedom. I've made a decision, consciously chosen my path, and for once it isn't based on following others. I feel an incredible lightness, as though my vessel has been cut adrift and I am its captain. I am at the helm of my life, no longer a follower but a leader simply by the act of choosing it. Now I really *can* do whatever I want.

I watch him pull on his boots and as he ties the laces a snowflake lands on them. I look up at the sky, at the white-grey clouds with the funny texture, at the fat flakes blowing down. We head back inside the hut and, wordlessly, Christian pulls out his sleeping bag and crawls into it.

By midday the clouds move on, leaving blue skies and white mountains, but the wind remains strong, whipping snow off the peaks. Again Christian readies to leave but I am still unsure. We have a big saddle to climb and the rest of the day remains at altitude. Are the clouds empty yet? It's nice here in the sun with these views. Maybe I should sit it out, hope the weather is better tomorrow.

The pain of getting caught out a few days ago is still fresh in my mind. It physically hurt. But then again, it *would* be nice to get moving. Perhaps if I rug up for it – get some layers on.

'I'll lend you my gloves,' Christian offers. 'They're windproof.'

'Done.'

~

Beyond the saddle a vast undulating valley is flanked by enormous bare mountains. Little flecks of snow turn into big flakes but now I am dressed for it, free to enjoy nature's drama. The gloves are invaluable and I marvel at Christian's gallantry. The snowflakes morph into balls of ice that sting my face and chest. They fly into my open mouth, crunching pleasingly when I press them between my tongue and teeth.

We make good time to Stone Hut and push on to the next, Bush Stream guiding us much of the way. We bash through slippery waist-high tussock, play 'spot the orange pole', and eventually the rusted corrugated iron box of Royal Hut appears, a grey dot in the middle of a barren alpine valley.

Inside it, two bench seats flank a metal table on a concrete floor. Eight bunk beds line the walls and a large stone fireplace waits invitingly, though there is not a skerrick of wood to be found and not a tree in sight. Someone has scrunched up tin foil to bog holes in the wall but the wind still whistles through, blowing snow into the corners of its wooden frame.

'*Royal* Hut, eh?' says Christian.

'Apparently Prince Charles and Princess Anne stayed here as kids.'

A clock sits on the mantelpiece, permanently stuck on twenty past four, and propped against the fireplace is a black guitar with two strings.

'Who *leaves* this stuff here?' I wonder. 'Ooh, I'll have that.' I say, suddenly spying a grey woollen blanket hanging over a bunk.

I need it. It's a cold night and I don't sleep well. The wind roars like a crazed beast, growing with intensity in the darkness, but despite its centenarian age the hut doesn't budge an inch. It's our hero, our protector.

The wind still roars in the morning. Christian risks a look outside to confirm what we already know. Neither of us is going anywhere.

The toilet is ridiculously distant, a telephone-box-sized cubicle stuck on a small ridge 300 metres away. Ventilation holes around its base let snow in, and balls of it fly around wildly like dollar notes in a competition cash booth. I hurry back to the hut to find Christian preparing breakfast. With the hood of his oversized black jacket cinched around his bearded face he looks more like a gnome than ever. I sit down opposite. Now we have a full day to watch each other do nothing.

He boils some noodles but the flavoured oil sachet has solidified. I watch him press it between the palms of his hands, warming it up. He gets out a cup, puts some sugar in it. He opens a ziplock bag full of tea bags and slowly pulls them out one at a time, holding each tiny bag with both hands and sniffing it before putting it aside to pull out the next one. Is he searching for a particular flavour?

Man, this is going to be a long day!

We sleep, we read – an assortment of *National Geographic* magazines and *Reader's Digests* left behind from the 1980s – and we talk. We do all this mainly tucked up in bed, the warmest place to be. I try to probe Christian for details about Liam, searching for some kind of insight, without arousing any suspicion that I care. Did he say why he skipped trail? Did he mention me? Christian doesn't know anything.

I get up, put on every item of clothing I have and dance, puffing clouds of condensation into the icy air. I jump and punch the air, trying to rev up my body. I've just spent all night horizontal and it won't be long before I have to do it again. Bounce. Bounce. Keep dancing. I eat a few nuts – not too many, though, who knows how long we'll be stuck here. I have a few squares of chocolate. Just for morale.

Outside, the wind continues to roar. The barometer on Christian's watch doesn't show any signs of movement. Night falls again and I lie in bed listening to music – Tiki Lounge, a compilation of 1950s bossa nova. Bongo drums, a small horn section, crooning voices, a softly rattling snare drum. I could be sipping cocktails on Ipanema Beach, watching tall and tanned and young and handsome boys walk by. I transport myself to another place – a warmer one.

I 'dance' in my sleeping bag until the song ends and roaring wind fills the gap, and in a jarring instant I remember I'm not on a beach in Rio but in a freezing hut high in the mountains of New Zealand. I giggle at the absurdity of it. Maybe I really am losing it.

~

I wake to silence but still there is fog and snow. The next leg is over Stag Saddle, the highest point on the whole trail. We need good weather. Not today.

I pace around the hut, poking around, looking for something to do. I've already scanned all the good bits from the magazines. My body aches. The mattress is hard. I dance around again then go back to bed. Sleep is the best way to pass the time.

I drift in and out, woken by the sound of the door creaking open. There's a gust of cold air, the shake of a jacket. I sit up expectantly. *Who's there?*

A rusty bearded face pokes through.

'Steve!'

'Oh, hey! How are ya?'

'Wow, good to see you! You're the most exciting thing that's happened today.'

'Brad's not far behind.'

The hut is transformed with laughter, music and new stories. Pots boil and steam fogs the windows.

I watch Steve try to get a tune from the two-stringed guitar. He's still cute but I've let go of trying to define us. It doesn't even seem to matter anymore – I've moved on, distracted by all the beauty around me.

The weather seems to be lifting. Christian's barometer is finally showing a rise. Maybe tomorrow.

Steve and I sleep next to each other, head to head. At seven I rock him gently. 'Time to get up,' I whisper. He slides up the bed, nuzzling a little closer, face almost touching mine. I throw my blanket over him and go outside. The chill air is still, the early morning sun skimming the snowy peaks. I want to get up there.

I pack quickly and make my escape. There is no trail but I weave back and forth across the river, climbing for hours towards the saddle. Somehow my socks are crunchy with ice, and the cold hurts.

I crest Stag Saddle and am blown away by the view. Aoraki, New Zealand's highest mountain, rises 3724 metres from a string of snow-capped ranges; to the south sprawls the vast distant blue of Lake Tekapo. It's undoubtedly the best view of the entire journey. I sit to wring out my socks, rubbing each of my numb feet, and finally the sun rises high enough to bathe me in its luxurious warmth.

'Yo!' Brad crests the saddle.

I turn to face him and then nod towards Steve, powering up a few hundred metres behind. 'Gee, he's looking strong.'

Brad grins slyly. 'He's probably trying to impress you.'

'It's working.'

'Hey, do we have reception here?'

I turn on my phone to find a message from Kiwi Scout. The nearby city of Christchurch just copped a hundred-year storm with about fifty houses drowned in floodwaters. He wonders how I have fared and I let him know we're all good.

We descend a ridge line together, joking and chatting, skipping over snow and shards of slate down to tussock plains. Christian stays at Camp Stream Hut but I push on with Steve and Brad, still flush with energy after two days of rest. A river cuts our passage, dotted with boulders, and Brad makes a leap for it. He pinballs from one rock to another, forwards, backwards, grasping at each but unable to land securely on any, and eventually comes to rest waist-deep in water. Without a word he climbs from the river and storms off down the track.

Steve and I stifle a laugh and walk on, side by side, through long grass the colour of burnt butter in the late sun.

'I missed you after Auckland,' he says. 'I wondered how you were going.'

'I'm glad we get to walk together again, even if it's only for a short while.'

'Oh, I reckon you and I will be walking into Bluff together,' he says quietly with a smile.

Waves of pink reach across a darkening sky. By eight there is plenty of flat ground and a rivulet of fresh water. It's all I need.

'I'm going to stop here.'

'Oh.' Steve stops walking too. 'Aren't you afraid of camping on your own?'

'No.'

'Well … Hey, Brad, what do you reckon?' he calls to the figure marching into dusk. 'We might as well stop too, eh? It's getting late.'

Our three tents line a high plain backed by distant white peaks. The skies turn purple, then blue and grey before surrendering to darkness. The ground is hard beneath me, no grass to soften it, no trees to mark it. The landscape stretches on like this for kilometres, immense, limitless. Empty but perfect.

I feel closer to the stars than ever, as calm as the still air, my potential as vast as the infinite black sky above. A great weight has been lifted from me. It seems I have the answers within, the capability – I am enough.

As a team of one, I made it through eight tough days since leaving Methven. I made it through the rivers, the tussock, the snow, over the mountains with no track. I got lost but I found myself again. I was cold, viciously cold, but warmth returned. I made mistakes but I learned from them.

I tried and I succeeded. And it wasn't that bad.

~

In a motel room in Lake Tekapo I have my first soak in a bath since Mary's house and the resulting surface scum is revolting, even to me. Grey skin cells clog my loofah mitt and clumps of long hair stick to my fingers. Yuck. I rub myself down with a towel but it just rolls off yet more dead skin. *What is happening to me?* I'm shedding layers, an entire skin, perhaps, like a snake. Soon there won't be anything left of the old me.

I study myself naked in the full-length mirror. It looks good from some angles, but not others. I have lost so much weight the skin sags slightly in places. I'm tired of thinking about my body. Maybe I'll just hide it for the rest of my life.

It dawns on me that without mirrors I had forgotten to search for my 'imperfections'. The daily ritual at home of staring at the reflection, turning sideways, judging myself, criticising. The memory makes me slightly ill. How unloving of me. This body that can do so much, that has faithfully carried me over 2000 kilometres despite all the challenges I've thrown at it. And I'm criticising it for how it looks.

I never realised how much time I spent worrying about what I ate or what my body looked like until it was no longer an issue. And in the months that I've been blissfully ignorant of how I look, I've wondered much less what others think of me. I've felt more real, felt my true essence shining through, free from any filters of self-doubt that might have influenced how I carried myself in the world or how I interacted with others. Anyway, even in my worst stink and grime – in one outfit, without makeup, my hair a mess – someone still found me attractive. Perhaps it doesn't really matter after all. Perhaps it's true what they say, that beauty is in the eye of the beholder, in the heart of the one who sees.

I dress and head to the hotel bar to pick up a newspaper. The front-page headline hits me like a sledgehammer to the gut. Civil protests in Kiev – sixty people shot dead by police snipers and at least a hundred more injured. I can scarcely believe my eyes. I turn the page – two brothers from North and South Korea selected by lottery for a one-off reunion after which they must part again. The photo shows two men, crying and embracing.

Are we humans all crazy?

The world's daily madness comes rushing back to consciousness, madness so common that in 'normal' life I probably disconnected from it to avoid its full emotional impact. For three months I have been shielded but now I am fresh again to its horrendous senselessness.

So much hate and anger in the world, so much noise and drama, pain and destruction – all man-made. It shouldn't be this way. I hang my head and a few heavy tears splash the page.

I wonder about my species. We seem deeply off track, hopelessly lost, like orphans who have never felt their mother's arms. Without any roots we wander, leaving a trail of destruction. Many of us try to fill a hole with power or possessions, shopping, food, alcohol, drugs, but it seems to me that such measures can only be a temporary balm if we do not cultivate inner happiness, wholeness and connectedness.

Immersion in nature has been my saviour. It's given me a connection to something much bigger than myself, given me perspective, roots, a solid base from which to live and grow.

But the world is busy undermining nature, destroying the very thing that can feed and nurture, the thing that makes me feel whole. Nature has no value in the modern economy – unless we can sell it.

We are displaced and we seem to be okay with it.

~

I have trouble getting to sleep. I lie in bed, admiring my room, a genuine seventies pad with bold, brown, circular-print wallpaper, orange boucle chairs and gold velour curtains. It's so retro it's cool. I turn the light out and lay in the dark, in a perfectly comfortable bed, feeling perfectly clean, perfectly full, and perfectly anxious.

Breathe!

I can't.

What's wrong?

I don't know.

What will I do if this thing never leaves me?

My mum wondered the same thing before I left home. I had tried to keep my pain hidden from her; I knew she would worry, and worry never helped anything. I needed peace, positivity. I didn't need questions clogging up my neurons. I didn't need to worry about a future that may or may not happen. I was trying just to get through the day, to survive the now.

My sister must have eventually told her, because Mum broached the topic over dinner.

'I'll be all right when I get on the trail,' I said, trying to close the conversation.

Her probing had been gentle to start with but her own panic seemed to take over. 'But what if you're not?' she asked. 'What about when you come home from the walk? What if you still feel like this then?'

New problems added to the raft of existing ones. I felt the waves rising around me, as I tried to stay afloat. I wanted to scream, to cry. Silently, I begged for her to stop.

'You've got a good job, you don't want to jeopardise that.' Her mind ran away with her, and dragged me along.

I just needed to hang in there, long enough so that I could reach the open spaces of the mountains and beaches, to escape to that place where I'd find the peace I so desperately needed.

~

Aoraki rises from a range of snowy peaks behind Lake Pukaki, milky blue with glacial sediment. I camp alone on its shores, gazing at the millpond calm that reflects roiling clouds of grey and white. My phone works. There's an email from Mum about my latest blog post, about the snowstorm, the trail-less route and the river crossings. She sounds in a panic. Where is Liam? And what about Christian?

Annoyance bubbles in my gut, molten magma.

'Please don't start any of your walks on your own, you *must* be with someone else as a safety precaution for all concerned,' she writes.

The volcano erupts.

For all concerned. What the fuck does that mean? For me? For her? Anyone else? What does my 74-year-old mother, in her armchair at home, know about the hike anyway? What does she know of the terrain, my skills, my experience now? Most hurtful is the assumption that whatever it is that I'm doing, I'm not capable of doing it on my own.

'At least two-thirds of the hikers I've met are solo! Why don't you think I can do it?' I stab the letters on my phone. I'm angry but I feel my throat tightening too. Her fear seems toxic. I can feel it poisoning my lightness, dampening my spirits. I don't care if it's generational. I don't care if it's love. It feels awful.

Suddenly it's clear – the pointlessness of fear, the damage it can do. I see how it limits, how it creates false borders, boundaries beyond which we dare not try. But I've ventured beyond those borders and I'm still here. Not only am I still alive, but I'm *more* alive! There is a whole new world beyond the boundaries of fear, and the walls that might once have limited me seem to be vaporising before my eyes. The more often I practise bravery the easier it becomes. The world is suddenly full of possibilities.

I breathe slowly and deeply, trying to shift my focus to the fierce love my mother holds for me – *don't take it personally* – a love so great it blinkers her from logic. She would do anything to protect me but the dangers she sees are based not on experience or knowledge. They are a creation of her imagination. Yes there are perils here but the risks can be managed – with knowledge, experience and with sound judgement.

I don't want to own this fear anymore.

On the lake shore I make a vow that I will not let fear be a part of my life, that I will recognise it when it appears and I will skirt around it, leave it behind. It's of no use to me. My decisions will be based on knowledge and a rational assessment of risk. I will listen to the voice inside, the one that gathers its knowledge from a thousand little pieces of information my conscious brain has neither the ability nor the time to process, senses and feelings unconsciously gleaned from my surroundings. Intuition.

Worry is pointless.

I try to find my centre again, to find that place where I am happy, where the world is open to me, but the email has unsettled me, threatening to return me to an old mindset. Come back happiness! Come back freedom!

I walk on, trying to ignore the niggle of anxiety that lurks a few steps behind. It's not just the email. There are only 500 kilometres left to hike. What happens after that? Antoine has been home for nearly a month yet still he struggles. 'I'm trying to adapt to my new life in the city but it's not easy to come back after so great a time and liberty,' he wrote.

A friend from home emailed, asking how I will assimilate into city life again. I don't *want* to assimilate. 'Ah, well, back to reality,' they say, as though I must return to the fold, conform, as though there is no other way. People are always saying to be realistic. I hate that phrase. Fuck being realistic! It simply means living within boundaries created by other people. Anyone who ever achieved anything great or new was not a realist.

There must be another way.

I recall the Māori words I read on a trailside plaque over 1000 kilometres ago: 'Look deeply and learn from your surroundings.'

Give it time, Laura. Wait for answers.

~

The track has no obvious ground trail for long stretches and the markers are often distant.

I walk into the remote Ahuriri River Valley, following a river carving between bare golden mountains. The trail notes are right, there aren't many trail markers, but I'm not bothered. I have food and shelter on my back. I am self-sufficient. I have no schedule, no demands. Time, as a notion, has ceased to exist. I want for nothing. I am free.

I realise how much I like walking alone, undistracted by conversations about work or favourite music or future travel plans. Silence is fertile ground for epiphanies.

Alone in a windswept valley I sleep. In the midnight hours curiosity nudges me to unzip the top of my tent flap and I gasp out loud at the sight of the Southern Cross constellation glowing brightly amongst a glitter of other stars. The universe, mind-bogglingly huge and beautiful – I feel it. The glow of the moon, the rush of the river – I can actually *feel* the vast expanse of the valley I lie in, and even the world beyond it.

There is nothing inside me in this moment. I am beautifully empty, and utterly complete. No pain, no noise. Opinions are irrelevant here. I am not what I do, what I wear, what I carry, what I look like. Anger has no place here, nor does fear, hate, judgement or ego, nothing that makes people want to hurt or control others. All stories have gone. I am free from the complications of being human. There is no chatter in my head, no tension in my soul. I am a house on a clifftop whose windows and doors have been left open, letting the breeze blow through.

I am elemental. No more than atoms that have been rearranged for millennia, in the rocks, the mountains, the animals and trees that surround me, part of the dead stars that everything on this planet is made of. I *feel* this connection. I feel the insignificance of my human story and the strength of my energetic vastness. The tussock dirt beneath me, the mountains, the river. I am *this*.

11

The Calm after the Storm

The Ahuriri River flows strong around my thighs. Beyond it is a flat plain with more mountains in the distance and I spend an hour being temporarily bewildered before picking up a vague trail. Drizzle turns to rain with a cold wind. My jacket steams from the exertion, leaving me hot and sticky yet chilly at the same time. I peak the rock and shale crest of Martha Saddle to face a headwind of freezing rain that looks fearfully white. *Please don't let it snow.*

With two plastic bags wrapped around my hands for protection, I descend to a hut as fast as I dare. A pair of boots dangle from a hook outside, and I push open the door.

'You're late,' says Christian.

'Sorry.' I grin back.

We walk together for a few days – river crossings, boulder hopping, sidling, all on exceptionally steep terrain. The final descent down to Lake Hawea drops nearly a kilometre of elevation in just two hours. Atop a knife-edge ridge, the ground ahead falls so steeply out of sight that I wonder where the track can possibly go. I peer over the edge to spy the tip of an orange pole jutting out of the jagged rock below.

Come on! Are you kidding me?

I know better than to worry now, though. Somehow, some way, I will get down there.

~

The track is exposed and follows a demanding line.
There are several steep sidles requiring care.

The Motatapu Track stretches between the two southern ski towns of Wanaka and Queenstown, and is full of vicious climbs and descents. Tree roots and rocks help me haul myself above the forest to open tussock, and there sits Fern Burn Hut, palatial with a shaded verandah on two sides and full-length steps cascading to a grassy terrace.

I crawl into my sleeping bag, legs bruised after yesterday's deep-tissue massage in Wanaka. Next to me, Christian's sleeping bag smells like a dirty dog. I lie awake listening to the sounds of sleep – hikers puffing, snoring, shifting in rustling nylon bags. I try to sleep but feel the tension rising, and the more I recognise it's there the more it grows, gathering in size and momentum like a rolling snowball.

My God, am I going to be right back where I started when I get home? Forever trapped in the grip of this awful thing?

I can't have it. It must go!

I press my eyes together and try to squeeze a few tears out

just to defuse the pressure but they're not ready to come.

What is this about? What's wrong?

I don't want to go back to filing systems and a noisy city, that much is clear, but right now I'm on a stunning New Zealand mountaintop. Why do I feel like this?

A voice arises in my mind, interrupting my thoughts. It's clear and certain: *I'm scared of not being me!*

And that's it.

A calm comes over me, like the clearing of the air after a rainstorm. A clarity, an honesty, as though I'm finally levelling with myself, finally listening to myself.

I fear living incongruently with who I am, of having to force myself into a box I know I don't fit. It feels unfair to ask my spirit to go back to the life waiting for me, dishonest to pretend I'm happy with it. I've heard its voice. My view has been expanded and this cannot be undone.

It's a relief to identify the cause of the conflict. I try to reason with the voice. Maybe I'm not trapped. No one's got a gun to my head. I've tackled this walk on my own, maybe I just have to continue being brave and follow my own path, wherever that may lead. Change isn't easy but there are options. I just need to find what it is that will make me happy. I need to find my route.

I reach for my diary and drag it inside my sleeping bag, pulling the cover over my head to block the light from my head torch, scribbling down thoughts and ideas, suddenly infused with energy.

I put my pen down to focus on sleep but a beam of bright light falls across my face from the window. The moon! Quickly

I roll to my stomach to stare at the brilliant ball of light rising above the dark mountains, slowly, slowly pulling away from the ridge. It lifts freely into the sky and intense joy flows through my body until my heart bursts with love. The moon, the mountains, the wind and grass, the lakes, the rivers, the birds and moss – all of this is what fills my heart with joy.

It seems impossible to fall asleep with the moon's light filling the valley and the excitement inside. I don't want to miss a second of it but a contented tiredness comes over me. As I drift off, I let the moon bathe my face and give comfort, just as I would the sun.

~

The ranges are like crumpled paper, screwed into a ball then roughly pulled open again, creating jagged peaks and valleys. I follow the high points, rising and descending along thin ridges, and in the emptiness my thoughts turn to Liam. I think of him a lot. Wishing I knew what the hell happened, why the fun suddenly ended. I needed to walk alone but still I feel sad about how our partnership ended.

Noon brings Highland Creek Hut. It's too early to stop but the next leg is long and demanding and heavy clouds are building. It's hard to muster enthusiasm for it. Maybe with some down time and a beautiful view I will be able to hear myself think, perhaps let more answers surface.

I struggle with the guilt of an afternoon off but a flick through the hut's visitor book shows I'm not the only one. What is it that drives us so relentlessly? It's as though an invisible stick were hovering at the ready. We're always pushing on just a bit further, a few more kilometres, over the next hill. I've seen hikers resist stopping for a snack break, the need to keep moving so great. Some have a deadline defined by a return flight but many hurry without seeming to really know why. It's as though we're programmed this way. Programmed to achieve – further, faster, quicker, lighter.

I see it in the city too. I did it myself. Working my way up the ladder because I could, because it's what we do. Striving, but for what? Where does it all end? When will we be satisfied? Have we been conditioned to *do* rather than *be*, our worthiness and success linked to how much we can get done and how fast we can do it?

Maybe our goal should be happiness. Maybe *that* is all we need to strive for. We're not here for long. If we're not squeezing as much joy as we can from life then what's the point? We should live every day, really *live* it. With gratitude. As though it might be our last – because it just might be. My dad taught me that. Why waste energy on petty concerns or false goals?

I decide I want to stop *doing* and start *being*. Being will ensure I am where I should be. Being is where it's at.

~

If the Arrow River is at normal to low flows then travel is quicker within the riverbed all the way to Macetown.

For nearly five kilometres I wade down the Arrow River across pebbles of shimmering green. It feels rebellious somehow. Surely only wild, crazy people walk through rivers for so long – without a marker in sight, without a track or companion. I'm forging my own way, making my own rules. I hoot out loud to enhance the picture of my madness and then laugh at myself.

Macetown is an old goldmining settlement, deserted for a hundred years. Cold, damp air sinks into the valley and stays there all night, turning my tent crispy and white. Shavings of ice bob about in my water bottle and it takes me half an hour longer to pack up as I defrost my fingers against the warmth of my belly.

A level trail cuts around the inside of the gorge. I can see it winding ahead, following the giant sweeping curve of the river. I zone out, lost in thought.

Then I notice in the distance a figure walking towards me. Tall. Solo. Dressed in khaki. The cogs in my brain falter slightly. Floppy hat. Front pockets.

Liam?

The figure moves closer, around the curving trail, and my heart pounds a nervous beat. It's definitely him. But here? Why? He should be heading south, far ahead of me.

In minutes our paths meet and there he is, in front of me.

'It's good to see you,' he says quietly, smiling.

We embrace, an awkward pack hug through two sets of front pockets.

'What are you doing here?'

'I've already been down to Bluff. I saw the weather was bad up here so I headed south to finish that first. Now I'm filling in the gaps. Doing the trail northbound through the mountains.'

'Right.'

We pause, a lull that holds so much unsaid, the guide ropes that defined our friendship now gone.

'I hope you forgive me for leaving,' he says.

'Oh …' I wave a hand dismissively, trying to think of something appropriate.

'You don't have to respond.'

'I just didn't want to do that section on my own. You had to do what you had to do.' I repeat the explanation he gave me a month ago, though it still doesn't ring true.

'I read your blog post about the snow.'

'Yeah. It was a bit of a challenge.'

We chat for a few minutes about nothing. Then we stand in silence.

'Well. I probably won't see you again, then,' I say.

'I guess not.'

We hug and squeeze past each other on the narrow trail.

I keep walking until a few minutes have safely passed and then turn around to watch the familiar figure in khaki, the one I followed for more than 1000 kilometres. Our goodbye has been rewritten, improved, but it's still unsatisfying. I have closure but no answers; the inner workings of his brain will remain a mystery.

He shrinks into the distance and I know it's the last I'll ever see of him.

~

South of Queenstown I enter a tussock valley flanked by mountains, the markers so intermittent I can't always see from one to the next. Te Araroa doesn't hold your hand. It assumes that you don't actually need a defined track and can cross rivers without the assistance of a bridge; trail markers, to Te Araroa, are just an occasional reassurance to your innate sense of direction and your solid map and compass skills. The trail is rugged, raw, uncontrollable and at times uncomfortable but it's taught me so much and its beauty and solitude have felt a rare treat.

I spot a tiny dot of orange hiding amongst the tall grass 50 metres away and veer gently towards it while keeping my eye on the bigger picture beyond, and it dawns on me how much things have changed. Being in the middle of a trackless wilderness without a pole in sight no longer induces a mild panic. Only four and a half months ago I left Cape Reinga, tight with anxiety and full of fears and unknowns. It's still so fresh in my mind yet at the same time seems ancient history. It's hard to reconcile the two states of mind. I've evolved into a different creature – one who's calm, capable and relatively at home in the wilderness. I have experience now, to find my way, cross rivers, make decisions. I know how to plan for enough food and water to see me through. Being temporarily bewildered no longer bothers me. I'm familiar with maps and can read the terrain. My GPS and I have a comfortable relationship. I know it won't always tell me the truth about where the route is, but it *will* tell me something about where I am based on my coordinates. Crucially, though, I don't *worry* anymore. I know I will find a way.

I'm also kinder to myself. Sometimes I make mistakes, but I see others make them too, and it's okay. Sometimes good decision-making gets us through and sometimes it's just luck. Either way I don't need to be so critical of my choices. If something doesn't work I can just make a change.

On summiting Everest, Edmund Hillary said, 'I'm sure the feeling of fear, as long as you can take advantage of it and not be rendered useless by it, can make you extend yourself beyond what you would regard as your capacity.' He's right. I can feel the change in me.

I needed the push. Had Belle never agreed to come with me I'd probably never have even tried. And without challenges I'd never have found out what I was capable of. I would never have had a chance to learn, to fail, to succeed, to grow. Safe options don't lead to epiphanies. For that you have to leap. You have to give up fear of failure, give up the quest for perfection.

Dark grey rain clouds loom behind me, the wind shaking clumps of tussock grass from side to side like cheerleaders' pompoms, ushering me on, to move quicker.

At Boundary Hut I fill in the visitor book: 'Laura Waters, party of one'.

The valley is all mine, a timeless space that challenges me to fill it. I sing at the top of my voice to the mountains and run across the dirt and grass, feeling almost drunk, though not a drop of alcohol has passed my lips.

The next morning is cold and wet and I manage only a few hours' walking before another hut lures me indoors. I light a fire and there is satisfaction in watching the gorse branches burn so feverishly bright, those vicious prickles that have scratched and thwarted me too many times to recall.

The rain passes, revealing fresh snow on the mountains. It looks cold. I walk outside for a temperature check. Yes, it is very cold. And, more importantly, I don't have enough time to walk 27 kilometres to the next hut. By nightfall it will be absolutely freezing.

The single bed against the window looks appealing, but the large 'dick and balls' someone has burned into the headboard seems like bad feng shui. I stake my claim in a dark corner instead, next to the fire. I have hours alone with my thoughts. I've only walked seven kilometres and the guilt of not *doing* has returned.

Steve, Brad and Christian arrive in the late afternoon, accompanied by Lucas, a young guy who barely speaks a word, and Roman, a friend of Steve and Brad who's joining them for the final few hundred kilometres. It's a full house. Chatter and music transforms the hut. Bloody bluegrass again. I almost wish for solitude.

'I don't blame you for staying here,' says Brad, throwing his pack next to the dick and balls bed. 'It's too cold to camp out tonight. I would have done the same thing.'

I walk nearly 60 kilometres over the next two days. Sheets of ice crust the tops of puddles, and I pass bushes full of red berries opaque with white crystals. Snow dusts the peaks in the distance and though the skies are clear I need to keep my beanie on until midday. The season is changing.

~

*'he ground trail is light, or non-existent, so care
and concentration are required to travel from
marker to marker. This makes the going quite slow.*

I leave the lakeside town of Te Anau with barely 300 kilometres left, the mountains shrinking and retreating behind me. The trail returns to forest, lush and moss-covered, undulating with slippery tree roots reminiscent of the North Island.

Stoat traps line the trails along with signs from the Department of Conservation warning of mass 1080 poison drops to kill pests – efforts to redress the natural balance. How much time and resources we spend trying to regulate and control other species, while overlooking the one major concern. An environmental pest might be defined as one that dominates its environment, squeezes out other species, one that changes and damages ecosystems, a population out of control. So who is regulating us?

Somehow we've never seen ourselves as part of nature, more a species separate, a species above, as though the rules for a balanced ecosystem don't apply to us. Instead we seek to control nature, to exploit and manipulate it for our own purposes, overlooking any havoc we might wreak along the way. Daily, across the world, we strip vast tracts of land of their trees, we raid the oceans of their fish, we pump toxic chemicals into the air and our drinking water, we throw so much rubbish into the waterways that there are garbage patches of suspended plastics in the Pacific, Atlantic and Indian oceans that are bigger than Texas. In the evolutionary blink of an eye we have altered the earth as surely as a plague of rabbits clearing a field of crops.

We are the tenants that wouldn't be getting our bond back. We have dug up the garden, torn down the curtains, burned the floorboards. What a mess we have made. I find it overwhelmingly depressing. Humans will reap what we sow but I feel for all the other species we're taking down with us, the mass extinctions forced by our hand. I think of the stupid excuses we make for our inaction on preserving the environment, on climate change, as though we can negotiate with Mother Nature. Nature doesn't give a toss about our reasons. It doesn't care about the economy or whether we think we can afford to make good our mess. The planet will go on. Maybe not in a form that will sustain us or even be recognisable to us, but it will go on, with or without us. For we are not the centre of the universe, we are just one part of it.

Our lives, often distanced from the natural environment, allow us to forget the bigger picture, to forget that we *need* this ecological balance, that it's only through the conditions of our environment that we have been able to become so successful in the first place.

But now I am *in* nature, really in it, immersed in a way I've never been before and in doing so I have emptied myself of the human story. No longer am I filled with political spin, advertising, societal influences or pressures. I am empty and, like a building left vacant for too long, nature has reclaimed me.

I've been rewilded, like the wolves of Yellowstone returned to their natural habitat. Reintroduced, they brought balance to a landscape that had become unbalanced. Perhaps if we can rewild humans, we too can redress the imbalance in our own environment.

I walk from forest to heavy tussock, chest high in places with the wind blowing in great gusts that push me sideways until I'm almost lying in the grass. On an open ridge I sit, watching the mist blow through the green and gold valleys below, and listen to the call of distant birds. It's impossibly beautiful. I wonder if one day we might rue our decisions, our greed, which led us to believe that this Eden wasn't enough.

For nearly an hour I watch and listen, serene, like some aged matriarch of the animal kingdom surveying her land. The balance in me has returned, my compass recalibrated. I know who I am now and what I want, though I don't yet know how to get it. I don't think I'd make the same mistakes, the ones I have made over and over. I don't think I'd choose the wrong man now. I certainly wouldn't stay with him.

My lust for Steve has transformed into fondness. He's brilliant but we're worlds apart. I think we both realise it. And do I really want to be with a guy who can't decide whether he's keen on me? No, I think a worthwhile relationship should look better than that.

And Liam. How could I ever get the deep connection I'm looking for with someone so closed? I want to be able to talk for hours, to laugh; I want someone enthusiastic, someone who can communicate.

I let go of the ties that bound me to these men like safety ropes I no longer need. I don't need a man to make me feel whole. Or friends and companions, for that matter. I don't have Belle, I don't have a partner, but for the first time in my life I have all of *me* and that is enough.

I breathe deeply.

In.

Out.

Peaceful. Grateful.

I'm grateful for my mother, who lives only to love her children. I turn on my phone to tell her I love her but there is no reception.

Slowly I make my way along the ridge, pausing to gaze at the views. Faint voices float on the breeze behind me and I turn to see Steve, Brad and Roman rise onto the distant ridge.

'Hi!' Steve yells out, waving.

'Hey there! Beautiful, eh?' I yell back.

'Have you had lunch yet?'

'No.'

'Wait there, we'll come over.'

I walk with them for the rest of the afternoon.

Steve and I sit in tall grass for a break.

'You've only got one now?' I ask, noticing the lonely, scratched red pole leaning against his pack.

'Yeah, I threw the other one across a river in frustration and ended up losing it.' He laughs. 'Didn't think it'd get swept away!'

Relaxed as ever. He's lost sunglasses, a hat, a pole and his way on numerous occasions, but never his positivity.

'Not far to go to the end now, hey,' I say, feeling a little sad.

'I know. What are you going to do after the walk? Hey, why don't you fly home from Auckland? I'll take you out for dinner.'

I smile, both of us knowing it'll never happen. 'Sounds good.'

We sit for a moment amongst the grass and the silent hills.

'Are you going back to work after this?' he asks.

'I don't want to. I hadn't really planned beyond the end of the hike. I sort of thought life would change, that I would have some big epiphany on the trail about what to do next but it hasn't happened.'

'Sometimes that comes later,' he says softly. Then another idea springs to mind. 'Hey, come and do some hiking in Korea!'

I laugh. That sounds good too.

~

It rains all evening. There is nothing to read so I lie in my tent and entertain myself with a slide show of my entire hike. Pictures scroll across the small display on my camera – Ninety Mile Beach, the forests, volcanoes, river gorges, mountains, people I walked with. Each photo prompts countless rich memories. Could all of this have happened in just five months? I look so round-faced at the start. My arms are fleshy. Steve doesn't have a beard.

An image appears and I dissolve into fits of tearful laughter for a full minute. It's of me, doing a 'river crossing' about two weeks from the start. It can't be more than ten centimetres deep. I stare at the smiling woman gingerly stepping out in her new hiking gear – naive, fresh-faced, oblivious to the challenges ahead. She seems from another time.

I'm a different person now. I couldn't be more different. I'm happy now, wiser and most definitely calmer. I'm someone who does cool shit. No filing systems, no writing office policies and procedures that no one will ever read. And yet now, less than a week from the finish, I fear I will lose this new person. Already some of the photos seem too long ago. The trail seems a brilliant but brief journey, like a comet, shooting into my life only to fly right past, leaving me in darkness again. I don't want to be deposited into the blandness of my old life. I must hold on to the feeling I have now. I am still this person.

I crawl out of my tent to brush my teeth, and bump into Steve. In the distant darkness an awful howl bellows out, like the moan of a zombie, making my skin shiver.

'Did you hear that?' says Steve. 'It's a stag. The roar is on.'

~

I've started having recurring dreams. I dream I'm still with Frank. I'm about to leave him and I'm repulsed that I'm still there. I can't believe I've stayed with him for so long. What was I *thinking* all this time? I wonder. My energy is uncoupled from his. I'm immune to his drama. I'm simply going.

It's not just Frank but other boyfriends too. Bad relationships left long ago that I haven't thought about in years. Where are these dreams coming from?

I wake in the middle of the night. Stags roar in the distance, and nearby is the soothing hoot of a morepork owl. In my semi-lucid state the sounds seem to wrap around me, to somehow become part of me. It's as though I can suddenly feel New Zealand, all of it at once, its essence interwoven with my very fabric. As though we are all connected, as one.

12

Finishing

The Longwood Forest is wet, saturated in green, a mass of rippled tree roots and big balls of moss clustered on tree trunks. At the distant edge of the forest I reach a sign: *Colac Bay 6 km / 2 hrs, Riverton 19 km / 6 hrs, Invercargill 51 km / 16 hrs, Bluff 88 km / 28 hrs.*

Twenty-eight hours. The end is now listed on directional signage. I have trouble comprehending it. After five months of solid hiking it will all be over in twenty-eight hours of walking, likely less.

Drizzling rain falls silently as I reach the beach and follow it for two days. Seagulls and oystercatchers congregate. Red seaweed and rubbery bull kelp lie strewn across the hard sand, which glistens with water, reflecting the grey sky above. The dunes look just the same as the ones up north, months ago. Even the weather casts the same light and colours. It's a familiar endless horizon and again I walk it alone.

Te Araroa is rewinding, back through mossy green forests, back along long empty beaches, the mirrored scenery at trail start and trail end sandwiching an almost incomprehensible number of experiences and change. I don't want it to end but the land has nearly run out. By tomorrow night the walk will be done.

I leave the beach to sleep in Invercargill, a busy hub of the south and a reminder of the world to which I will soon return. Cars and people move at speeds I'm not used to and the pavement somehow feels dirtier than the earth of the trail – sticky with day-old soft drink and wads of dried chewing gum, empty burger wrappers blowing on the wind.

Steve sends me a text from a campground on the edge of town.

We're going to leave early tomorrow morning. I'll send you a message when we're packed up and ready to go.

Thanks. I can't believe it's nearly over, I reply.

I know. How ya feeling about it?

Feeling a bit flat actually, a bit sad.

Yeah. Me too.

~

His message comes at 6.30am. I power-walk through the dark streets to find Steve, Brad, Roman and Lucas scoffing hot pies at a roadside takeaway on the outskirts of town. The mood is festive. This is it – the final 30 kilometres to Bluff.

We walk together as a team, marching single file on the hard shoulder of a highway, talking and laughing. Cars pass at 100 kilometres per hour and some toot and wave. No one but a thru-hiker would be walking this road verge. It occurs to me that we must look clean and fairly normal to a passing stranger but they would have no idea of the trials we have faced to get here. The mud we've slid on, the gorse we've bashed through, the steep, sweaty hills, freezing snowstorms, the rock scrambling and precipitous trails. They wouldn't know of the tears, blood, blisters and aching muscles or of the thousand-plus hours of hiking that it took. God, what a journey. I've loved it.

We leave the highway to skirt the rocky headland – the bluff – the final seven kilometres. The Southern Ocean spreads before us, blue in a way that only comes with clean, deep water. Waves crash over the rocks, clumps of kelp swirl in rock pools, the mid-autumn sun warms us. It's perfect.

Our pace slows. We stop regularly, to snack, to admire the views, to savour our last steps. Suddenly we have all the time in the world. No longer do we hurry to get somewhere. We're already here.

I round a bend and see it – the multi-pronged yellow sign that marks the trail's official end. Sitting in the middle of a modest platform on the edge of a car park, it looks much smaller than I expected. It's a subtle finish line for such an epic hike but it matches my mood.

I had tried to envisage this moment long before I ever started. How would I feel? Elated? Tearful? Proud? Exhausted and never wanting to hike another step again? I feel none of these. The end comes quietly, simply a natural progression in nearly half a year of walking. It's what we do.

We celebrate the achievement but not so much the end. Arms are raised, moments of glory captured on camera, and then another few kilometres of walking to the tiny township nearby to find a pub.

Steve pokes his head inside a store. 'Is it Tuesday or Wednesday today?' he asks.

'Monday,' comes the faint reply from inside.

The pub is near empty. I order champagne while the boys down beers. We take it in turns to drop coins into the jukebox and sink into a hazy state of celebration.

I'm happy. I'm fit, strong and happy. But I can't comprehend where I am. It's as though I've suddenly lost steering. Every minute of the last five months has had a purpose, all driving me to this moment, but now what?

For a few weeks I've been sending emails to Ben, asking when exactly he expects me back at work, and as I sit in the pub, champagne in hand, I finally receive a reply.

'Please return when you are ready. I am just grateful you wish to come back.'

I don't wish to.

'You're so lucky to have a boss like that,' Steve says, swirling the last of his beer around his glass before knocking it back.

Hours later we stagger into the cold night air to find the campground, clutching slabs of beer and hiking poles, bouncing off each other and singing loudly. We get a cabin just large enough for us all and pile inside. Brad pulls out his speaker one last time and the celebrations continue until none of us can keep our eyes open and the drunken snoring begins.

Two of us need to share the one double bed in the room. Steve pulls me close in the darkness, all big beard and bushy hair.

He's a lot hairier than in Wellington. It's snuggly. We kiss and he holds me tightly all night.

In the early hours he gives me a hug and a kiss and is gone, on a plane to Auckland.

~

I'm not ready to stop walking.

Brad and I cruise the Foveaux Strait to Stewart Island, our goal Doughboy Bay. The most southerly part of the island, and therefore New Zealand, that can be reached by trail, it seems a fitting place to hang up our boots.

It's an easy 14 kilometres to North Arm Hut, which is heaving with excited hikers. People ask me questions, speak loudly, move noisily. It's all perfectly normal but my chest tightens anyway.

We push on west, leaving the crowds behind, past beaches and bays, moss-covered forest, mud and streams. In the island's centre, a long tunnel of manuka bush opens out onto swamp plains with expansive views of distant mountains, and I feel the familiar peace and space, the calm returning – nature's drug gliding into my veins.

It takes ten hours to reach the west coast and when Mason Bay Hut comes into view I suddenly feel very lazy. It looks like a beach house, quietly nestled at the base of the sand dunes, a few faded pink and blue buoys dangling from palms outside. The late afternoon sun bathes it in a warm glow, beckoning me to relax. Maybe I won't even go to Doughboy. I want to stop and enjoy my surroundings.

This is it.

I've walked enough.

~

The thought of going home fills me with confusion and dread, like some bad dream that surely cannot be real.

Who am I now? Where is my path from here?

The trail has stripped me of my identity. I have let go of my story, of everything I thought to be true about myself. The lies said to me once, which I repeated over and over, keeping them alive so that they tainted everything I did – that I was unwanted, incapable, not good enough, that I had to live my life a certain way, that I must continue my existence alone and apart – they have gone, leaving behind a blank slate.

There is no way I can fit into my old life now, my old lie. I know what happiness feels like. I have a new measuring stick by which to gauge it. I don't want to numb my spirit into just existing again. I have been living, *really living* – raw and real.

I want to stay here, the fibres of my being interwoven with the earth, the trees, the water, the sky. I have managed to find my way back to nature, where I feel supremely at peace. I don't want to leave.

13

Home

I return home.

I find a room to rent, an hour's walk from the city, the first place of my own since I broke up with Frank eighteen months ago. I go back to work. There are more corporate meetings, earnest talk of future plans. The filing system has gone haywire in my absence but I don't care anymore.

Dave opens the desk drawer between us, gesturing for me to dig into his stash of Haigh's chocolate. 'You're swearing more since you came back.' He studies me with a smile. 'You're funnier too.' He knows something has changed, something irrevocable. 'You want to write this book? Just *go!*'

'But what about the job?'

'Don't worry about it!' He waves a hand dismissively. 'You'll get another one later.'

I've always liked his confidence. His belief in himself has always made the insane seem possible. And now he's extending that confidence to me.

I've always wanted to write. When I was ten I bought myself

a thick spiral-bound notebook in which to pen a novel but found myself paralysed by its empty pages, and so I let the idea go. But now, thirty years later, the urge to create has returned. I want to do it as a project just for me, to have a go, just to say that I've finally done it.

I head out to meet a friend for lunch in a sleek concrete courtyard amidst the skyscrapers. Our conversation is interrupted by the beep of his phone. 'I've got sixty messages to check just from this week,' he groans. 'That, on top of the six hundred emails I haven't even opened yet!'

In what kind of world is this okay? I wonder. His company has a new internal tagline: *Ambition, Achieve*. It prods its workers, keeping them focused on the corporate machine and distracting them from their lives beyond it.

I gaze around at the other tables. Sunlight catches on glossy, tong-straightened hair; fake eyelashes flutter on carefully contoured faces. I never really noticed it before. How long does it take these women to get ready in the morning? How might the world be different if they let their natural beauty shine instead? I think of my friend Melanie – twenty-nine, stunning and using botox. It seems madness.

I can no longer relate to life here, to the people around me. The rituals of work, of pub-drinking, of shopping – there is no satisfaction in it anymore. I yearn for something that feels meaningful yet I struggle to find it. Social media overflows with curated and orchestrated images – of pouting lips, tilted heads, of people trying to look cool. There are photos of islands and mountains with colours ramped to the max as if nature wasn't beautiful enough. There are images of camping trips, of saggy tents perched on exposed cliff tops, lone girls with flowing hair, backs turned to the camera. No one would ever camp there, just as no one would hike in skinny jeans, an oversized canvas jacket and a trilby hat. It's only for show. I read a disturbing statistic of the importance of 'Instagrammability' to young travellers. It seems we no longer travel to see – to learn or discover something new – but to *be* seen.

I feel so outside of things; at every turn there's something that jars. I watch the evening news and see two men in fluoro vests wrestling on a car bonnet, a road rage incident captured on a dash cam. Flicking through the channels, I skim snippets of reality TV packed with more anger, drama and tears, and recognise that, weirdly, it has been manufactured that way. I can't understand why there seems such a hunger for it. Hateful comments on the internet are shocking to me. Judgement seems to come quickly; compassion, kindness and understanding less so. I've gone from months of peaceful meditation to a bunfight. What the *hell* is going on?

The walk shielded me, kept me blissfully unaware of current affairs, but now, faced with media on the state of politics, I'm left feeling lost and helpless. Parliament seems more like an episode of *Survivor* than a place of wisdom and leadership, with participants doing what they think they must do to win, not what is fair and right and reasonable. There is talk of reducing marine parks so that more fish can be pulled from the sea, of felling ancient trees in Tasmanian forests, of mining on the Great Barrier Reef. What are they doing to my precious planet?

The need for new underwear forces me on a mission to the local shopping centre. Already the largest in Australia, it has expanded yet again in my absence, its vast and shiny halls lined with banks of TV screens flashing colour and noise; adverts competing with loud music. It's like a casino. A billboard shows a handsome man punching the air. 'Get that new phone feeling every year!' On another there's a girl with a flawless figure in a yellow bikini, asking whether I am 'beach body ready'. *I was born ready!* I want to shout. *We all were!*

I have become an outsider, an observer. This is no longer my world. Nature calls to me, beckoning me to return. *You know this is where you are happy*, it says. *Remember how amazing you felt? How alive? You were full of ideas and energy here, full of hope. Do you really want to let that go?*

I walk home from the office in the dark of a winter's evening and notice the full moon glowing above the streetlights. It is the same moon I saw from that hut on the Motatapu Track. If I draw a line now from me to the moon and then back down to another location where its beam is shining, it will lead me back to a quiet place with a soft wind blowing through an open hut door, tussock glowing silver in the half light. It's still there, now, even though I am here. It's still real.

That moon leads me back to rivers and mountains, to peace and quiet.

Back where I belong.

14

One Giant Leap

My sister bangs about the kitchen, glaring at me with eyes afire between bouts of throwing around utensils. She's impatient. She's been waiting a week to hear what I have to say. The family are gathered at her house for dinner – her husband, my nephews, one friend, my mother. I planned it this way.

'You've got a new job,' she barks out, a wild guess.

'No,' I say.

'You're pregnant!' she tries again.

'Are you?' My mum claps her hands together, face lit with joy.

'No! What?' I look at her, exasperated. 'Geez, Mum! I don't even have a boyfriend!'

'Well what is it?' My sister will wait no longer.

I take a deep breath. 'I am quitting my job. I'm moving to an island in the Solomons to do some volunteer work with a little resort. A few hours' work a day in exchange for food and accommodation.' I bring up a photo on a tablet to show them a picture of my new home in the South Pacific, a thatched wooden bungalow perched on the edge of a shimmering coral lagoon –

Oravae Cottage. Quickly I outline the plan, keen to sell the idea before anyone can challenge its worth. 'I want to write this book and I'm too tired to be creative at night after sitting in front of a computer all day so I'm just going to take some time out for a year to focus on this project.'

I announce it to the family as one, relying on an overall positive response to balance out my mum's inevitable resistance. Hoping that, because everyone else does, she might see it as something exciting, as something worthwhile, and not just that I am leaving my safe, 'good' job.

The room erupts in wows and envious *oohs* and *ahhs*.

'Oh my God, is that bungalow going to be your *home*?'

'When do you go?'

'How big is the island?'

Mum watches the excitement, taking the scene in, eyes twinkling.

'How wonderful,' she says.

~

I lasted four months before I handed in my resignation. I sat down in Ben's office just before five, wondering how to phrase it, how to tell him – the best person I'd ever worked for – that I was leaving. We sat there looking each other for a few long seconds.

'Do you know what I'm going to say?' I winced, hoping he might let me off the hook by guessing.

'Time to go?' he asked softly.

'Yeah.'

He got it. He always did.

It seemed crazy that I might give up this job – the stable one with the comfortable salary, great team and a free ski-lift season pass – but I had decided to live my life from the heart, allow *it* to call the shots, and this suddenly made things very clear.

I would live simply to go work on my book, my passion. I would throw all rules out the window to follow my dream in the ultimate leap of faith. It felt exhilarating, to *throw off the bowlines,* to *sail away from the safe harbour*, as the quote goes. Destination unknown.

~

Six weeks after the family dinner I sit on a plane, jetting across the Pacific. The flight attendant hands me an immigration form. I fill in my name, my address, my nationality, but one question gives me pause – occupation. I hover my pen over the little boxes. I am not employed but I do have a job to do. *No one's going to challenge you on this, Laura.* I feel a thrill rush through my body as I enter the letters – WRITER.

The island is hot and tiny. It takes me three minutes to walk its length and thirty seconds to cross its width. For two months I mix a few hours' work a day with writing, and the isolation forces my focus. Each day I snorkel around the island, saying hello to the sharks, trevally, lionfish and giant clams that I pass. It's a simple life. Quiet. An enforced meditation. I write 40,000 words and then throw them all out after a friend back home informs me the average book is less than double that, and I had only documented up to day eight of my journey.

But I've made a start. The wheels are in motion.

No longer am I too afraid to try.

Epilogue

Little Penelope paws at my leg, asking to be lifted as I type at the laptop on the kitchen table. A gorgeous featherweight mongrel of black fluff, she's only known me a few days but we've bonded well.

'Are you okay, Toby boy? Toby, Toby, *Toooobyyyyy?*' I cast some verbal love towards the blue heeler curled on a bed in the corner. He raises a sleepy eyelid in response.

I flew to Adelaide a few days ago, where I was collected by strangers and driven to this house so that I could look after their dogs and water their garden while they travel overseas. I can't afford to rent my own property but that's fine with me. Owning things costs money and possessions just tie me down.

When I returned from Te Araroa two years ago I looked at my bedroom, held for me in perpetuity at my mother's house, and I couldn't believe how much *stuff* it contained. How had I, a reluctant shopper at best, managed to accumulate so much of it? New Zealand had taught me that I could manage five months with just one outfit and one bag of belongings, and the truth of it is that I'd never been happier. Simplicity, it seemed, was the key, so on my return I set about getting rid of things. I sold stuff on eBay to fund my new lifestyle and recirculate goods that I no longer used. Spare bikes in the shed I hadn't used for years, clothes that were always left on the hanger while I reached for old favourites. It felt good to clear the clutter and even better to earn some cash. Now I travel with about half-a-dozen outfits – anything I can't comfortably fit in a backpack is too much.

House-sitting suits me well. There's always a sense of discovery when you regularly wake up in new locations. Today it's Victor Harbor, a sleepy seaside town on the stunning Fleurieu Peninsula in South Australia. My day began with throwing balls for the dogs on a peaceful, sun-kissed beach, where the locals greeted me with easy smiles and waves. This afternoon I will take Penelope and Toby somewhere else. Maybe a hike along the top of the Waitpinga Cliffs – part of the long-distance Heysen Trail – or maybe a jaunt around the granite boulders and blue ocean views of The Bluff. I will not get bored here, that's for sure.

On the table in front of me is the latest hiking magazine, opened at a story I wrote about a solo hike on the 250-kilometre Great South West Walk in Victoria. There have been numerous other stories before it. I even made the cover a few times. Once was for the publication that first alerted me to Te Araroa's existence; I was pictured near the top of the Waiau Pass.

Writing hasn't been easy. I've had to learn from scratch, and the pay is rubbish, but for the first time in my life I am doing something I'm genuinely passionate about. Plus, I can kind of justify hiking as 'work'.

It's a far cry from my old life. I've long forgotten that horrible feeling I had every single morning when the alarm went off, when a little part of me would die inside as I considered the commute and the office ahead. When I lived only for evenings or weekends. Now, instead of board minutes and risk assessments, my computer screen shows maps and planning notes for the new Kangaroo Island Wilderness Trail, which I'll embark on in a few weeks' time.

I've been walking a lot recently: the Great Ocean Walk in Victoria, stuffed with sea views and koalas, then the Larapinta Trail in the Outback, over red earth, dry riverbeds, gorges and mountains. I headed back to New Zealand's South Island, knocking off the popular Abel Tasman, Kepler and Routeburn tracks, plus the more challenging Gillespie Pass Circuit, Cascade Saddle route and Hokitika track.

While I was there I spent a few months volunteering at a forest camp in Hanmer Springs, cleaning toilets and stacking firewood for a few hours a day in exchange for my own little cabin. It was the perfect place to write and, in my afternoons off, I got to hike amongst my beloved beech forests and craggy mountains.

I met a man there too – a nice one. I was sitting on the deck of a hostel in Wanaka, gazing out towards its alpine lake and mountains, when I noticed him. He was barefoot and tanned with short silver hair; his eyes were dark chocolate pools. Pages of *War and Peace* went fluttering off into the breeze from the copy he'd been reading and our laughing attempts to retrieve them were enough to strike up a conversation.

He was an adventurer like me, seeking a life less ordinary: halfway through sailing around the world on a yacht. He was a glider pilot, a skilled archer, a mountaineer who'd scaled Mont Blanc. He was a business owner from London, with a plum accent to match. He looked as though he belonged in a Rolex advertisement.

It didn't last but for eighteen months I shared love – a proper, respectful, loving kind of love – with a man who adored my body. For six weeks we sailed up the Queensland coast, then hiked and toured together on land. I think he was the first adult I'd ever dated.

Life certainly entered another dimension after I quit 'reality'. From my desk in Melbourne I could never have imagined all the things I would do, the people I'd meet and the places I'd go. I could never have foreseen all the opportunities that were open to me from that one static point. But change creates new thinking and new thinking creates new possibilities. In taking the leap I've done all the things I wouldn't have done if I'd listened to my brain – a brain that knew only what it had learned, what it had been told, what other people thought, a brain that favoured the standard line, the well-worn path, the 'safe' option.

Though I didn't have much of a plan when I quit my job, I at least knew which track I wanted to be on and that, I have discovered, is usually enough. Just one step in the right direction and the rest will unfold in good time. Happiness and inspiration are my guides now. At any crossroads I simply ask myself, *Does this feel good?* And, really, that is the bottom line.

Though I give ultimate control to my gut now, I could never have trusted its opinions three years ago. Its view was tainted by society, by early programming. I had to connect with my authentic self first – to really know myself – and only by sitting quietly for so long could I lose all the noise and hear the true voice beneath.

There are no regrets now, even for the few compromises that have been necessary. I earn a fraction of what I did before and sometimes it's a challenge. Movies and dinners out are rarities. But in place of money I have freedom and it makes me feel unbelievably rich. I've discovered that if I don't spend a lot of money I don't *need* a lot of money. In living simply, I've watched many of my bills simply dry up. The car I gave up before Te Araroa hasn't been replaced. There have been no more train tickets to an office in the city or gym memberships to stay fit. There is no sprawling wardrobe to update or need for regular splurges at the day spa to relax. My whole *life* is relaxed. I am careful not to fill it – I don't want to be so busy that I might forget who I am or where I am headed. I avoid busy places and unnecessary drama and the lack of these things creates space for more positive things – for thought, contemplation, creativity. The silence allows me to find the answers that are already within.

I still occasionally experience a tightness in my throat, a shortness of breath, but now I take heed of the discomfort within my body. I see it as nature's way of getting my attention. If you lean on a hot stove, pain will tell you to pull your hand away before you do damage to your cells. For me, emotional pain is the same – nature's way of saying, 'Hey! We've got a problem! You need to change something here!' Now when I feel that tightness in my throat I stop and listen to my body. I say, 'I hear you. It's okay. We're going to fix this.' And almost immediately I can feel it responding, a relaxing and releasing.

Happiness is important; only by being whole in ourselves can we best contribute to the whole. An unhappy soul has little to spare for others, but an inspired one, filled with energy and enthusiasm, knows no bounds. It will smile, have more patience, support and love more freely.

I have a mission now – to encourage others to spend more time in nature, to feel its soothing presence and hear its wisdom. I want others to reconnect with it, cherish it and to realise the joy that can be found in simplicity. I don't know exactly how I will make this happen or where it will all lead – maybe nowhere. I'm a beginner, like the relatively inexperienced hiker I was, launching myself on the trail in Cape Reinga. I'll just give it a go. See how far I get.

I stroke Penelope's soft fur, feeling her little pink tongue lick my hand.

My pre–Te Araroa life seems crazily distant now – another time, another world. The recurring dreams about Frank that I'd had towards the end of my hike were probably representative of my larger life. The city life and the office work that I hated – why did I stay with them for so long when they weren't making me happy? Why did I think I couldn't leave them? What on earth was I *thinking*? `

This is my world now.

My story.

Just as I choose to write it.

Author's Note

This is a true story. All of the events are authentic. However, in some areas the timeline has received a minor massage for the purposes of keeping the story moving, and some scattered moments have been condensed into single scenes to spare the reader unnecessary boring bits. The names and descriptions of some characters and backstory locations have been changed to protect the privacy of those involved. Dialogue is as recalled and noted in copious diary entries.

Acknowledgements

If I ever thought hiking the length of a country required grit, stamina and determination, it was nothing compared to writing a book about it. I'd like to thank the many people who supported and encouraged me throughout this epic challenge, and helped me to realise a lifelong dream. In no particular order…

Thank you to New Zealand and your people for allowing me such an amazing journey. Thank you for healing me, for your beauty, hospitality and everything you've taught me. You changed my life. I'm deeply grateful to Geoff Chapple for having the vision to create the Te Araroa Trail in the first place, to the Te Araroa Trust for managing it – including providing those invaluable maps and trail notes – and to the many volunteers who continue to contribute to this epic route. Thanks to the landowners who allow us hikers to walk across your fields and follow your fence lines. I'm indebted to the Department of Conservation for maintaining the trails (okay, maybe not all of them but I know it's a budget thing) and providing such an utterly wonderful backcountry hut system – long may it continue. Those sheds and palaces were a haven in tough times. There is truly no happier place for me than in a hut in the wilds of New Zealand.

Thank you Belle Tozer for agreeing to come with me on this crazy jaunt in the first place – you got me where I needed to be – and for your ongoing friendship. I'm so grateful to everyone I shared time with on the trail, for the laughs and the interesting conversations, particularly 'Steve', 'Brad', 'Antoine', 'Liam', 'Isabel', 'Summer' and 'Christian' – you guys know who you are. You all enriched my journey and made it so much more enjoyable. Thanks to the many trail angels who came to our aid by offering a hot shower, somewhere to put up a tent, rides from the trailhead to town for resupplies, fresh vegetables from the garden or homemade biscuits. Special thanks go to Mary Johnston for making me a birthday cake, and to Jeff Hermes, general manager of the Kingsgate Hotel in Wellington, for supporting my stay there.

I am deeply grateful to Nick Whitby for being the incredibly supportive boss that he was during my entire time working with him before the hike, and particularly during the difficult later days when I was struggling. Thanks for your understanding and patience, and for letting me go. Massive thanks to Darren Walls for being a great mentor and encouraging me to follow my heart – you're awesome. I'm grateful to everyone who supported me post-hike and reassured me that quitting a regular job to follow my dream wasn't a crazy thing to do – in particular Liza Smith, Kylie Wealands and Belinda Reid. I'm also indebted to the many friends and family members who have so kindly subsidised me during the frugal writing process with a lunch or dinner here and there. I hope to pay you back soon!

Writing a book has been a huge learning curve. Lisa Cron, I've never met you but your book *Wired For Story* gave me crucial insights on where to begin. Putting your story down on paper is a soul-baring process and I'm very grateful for the gentle encouragement of friends who read various drafts and gave supportive and constructive feedback, in particular Jane Crouch and Craig Elder. Craig, you've been an amazing friend and mentor throughout this whole process. Thanks for your wisdom and guidance, and thanks for hooking me up with all your Kiwi mates. Thank you Miranda Daniels for being my one-woman cheerleading team whenever I've doubted myself.

Thomas Ryan, your feedback and encouragement meant a lot and kept me hopeful during the long and, at times, challenging writing process. Thanks also for connecting me with your wonderful editor Cate Hogan for those early rounds. Cate, I can't begin to thank you enough for the education you have given me and for delivering your feedback in such a kind and encouraging way. When all felt helpless and overwhelming, you kept me on track and reassured me that I could do it.

I'm eternally grateful to the gorgeous Ruby Ashby-Orr at Affirm Press for 'discovering' my manuscript at a literary speed-dating event. Thank you so much for your support and gentle feedback that helped craft the book in its later stages, and also thanks to Emma Schwartz who guided me during the manuscript's final polish and made sure I didn't say anything too outrageous (I hope!).

Sincere thanks go to the entire team at Affirm Press for being so great to deal with, and for their guidance through a process that has been completely new to me. In particular, Martin Hughes and Keiran Rogers for taking me on and giving me a go, and to the lovely Laura McNicol Smith for helping me get the word out there.

Hiking can be miserable without the right gear and I am indebted to British equipment manufacturers Rab for providing me with such awesome kit. Your thermals, fleece, hiking pants, waterproofs, down jacket and sleeping bag not only looked good but performed brilliantly, easily lasting the distance under some pretty testing conditions. Sincere thanks go to Brian Thurston for arranging everything. I'm also grateful to Bogong Equipment in Melbourne for their expert advice when I knew nothing about preparing for a long hike, and for their assistance with camping gear. Backpacking Light in Melbourne have also been supportive, and for this I thank Tim Campbell. Thanks also go to Air New Zealand for flying me to Kaitaia to begin the trail.

Finally, but not least, I'm grateful to my family. Thank you Mum for your unconditional love and for giving me a roof over my head whenever I need one, even in my adult years! You have always supported me. Thanks also to my sister, Cheryl, and my brother, Mat, for always being there. And finally, thank you, Dad. Whatever eloquence I may have managed to nurture, it came from you.